W  TION

How To Books on Successful Writing

Awakening the Writer Within
Copyright & Law for Writers
Creating a Twist in the Tale
Creative Writing
How to Be a Freelance Journalist
How to Publish a Newsletter
How to Start Word Processing
How to Write a Press Release
How to Write & Sell Computer
  Software
Improving Your Written English
Making Money from Writing
Mastering Business English
Publishing a Book
Researching for Writers
Starting to Write
Writing About Travel
Writing a Non-fiction Book
Writing a Pantomime

Writing a Report
Writing a Textbook
Writing an Assignment
Writing an Essay
Writing & Publishing Poetry
Writing & Selling a Novel
Writing Business Letters
Writing Erotic Fiction
Writing for Publication
Writing for Radio
Writing for Television
Writing Historical Fiction
Writing Humour
Writing Reviews
Writing Romantic Fiction
Writing Science Fiction, Fantasy &
  Horror
Writing Short Stories and Articles
Writing Your Dissertation

Other titles in preparation

The How To Series now contains more than 200 titles in the following categories:

Business & Management
Computer Basics
General Reference
Jobs & Careers
Living & Working Abroad

Personal Finance
Self-Development
Small Business
Student Handbooks
Successful Writing

Please send for a free copy of the latest catalogue for full details (see back cover for address).

SUCCESSFUL WRITING

WRITING FOR PUBLICATION

How to sell your work and
succeed as a writer

Chriss McCallum

4th edition

How To Books

Cartoons by Mike Flanagan

British Library Cataloguing in Publication Data
A catalogue record for this book is available from the British Library.

Published by How To Books Ltd, 3 Newtec Place,
Magdalen Road, Oxford OX4 1RE, United Kingdom.
Tel: (01865) 793806. Fax: (01865) 248780.

First edition 1989
Second edition 1992
Third edition 1995
Fourth edition (revised) 1997
Fifth impression 1998

Note: The material contained in this book is set out in good faith for
general guidance and no liability can be accepted for loss or expense
incurred as a result of relying in particular circumstances on statements
made in the book. Technical and legal matters are complex and liable to
change, and readers should check the current position with the relevant
authorities before making personal arrangements.

Produced for How To Books by Deer Park Productions.
Typeset by PDQ Typesetting, Stoke-on-Trent, Staffs.
Printed and bound by Cromwell Press, Trowbridge, Wiltshire.

Contents

List of Illustrations

Foreword

My delight at being invited to write a foreword to this book is tempered only by the fact that it really doesn't need one. Just glance at the list of contents or flick through the pages at random and you'll quickly realise that here is a general guide for the writer – and particularly the novice writer – as valuable as the *Highway Code* is to the motorist.

Totally free of waffle; packed with good, solid advice and information; entertaining, instructional *and* encouraging all at the same time. A really excellent choice as a 'starter' book for any aspiring writer and a more than useful addition to the shelves of even the most professional one. It is, quite simply, one of the best books of its kind that I've ever read.

Steve Wetton
Author of BBC TV's comedy-drama *Growing Pains*

Preface
to the Fourth Edition

You want to write, and you want to get your writing published. Where do you start?

THINGS YOU NEED TO KNOW

- What to write.
- How to write it.
- Where and how to sell it.

You need a guide

It's a bit of a maze, this writing business. You'll be surprised how big it is, too. It's no use wandering about on your own. You'll only waste time and effort – and money.

Try to resist the itch to pick up a pen or plug in your keyboard till you've taken the round trip. You'll be ready then to decide which point of entry you want to try first.

Feedback from earlier editions tells us that fiction writing is the most popular of all the writing fields. This edition, like the second and third, includes detailed constructive advice on criticising, revising and editing you own work.

Don't disregard the other options, though. There's ten times more non-fiction than fiction published today, and there's no reason why you shouldn't write both.

Acknowledgements

For permission to publish original quotes, copyright material and personal experiences, the author and publishers thank Alan Bond, Patricia Brennan, Wally K Daly, J T Edson, Peter Finch, Robert Goddard, Robbie Gray, Paul Heapy, Joan B Howes, Ted Hughes, H R F Keating, Joyce Lister, Brian Lumley, Dorothy Lumley,

11

Harry Mulholland, Mike Pattinson, Peggy Poole, Ken Rock, Jean Sergeant, Liz Taylor, Graham Thomas, D C Thomson & Co Ltd, Gordon Wells, Steve Wetton and Charles R Wickins.

Note

Editors and publishers, like writers, spring from both sexes. If anyone can invent a workable device to convey that fact neatly and without the awkward use of 'he or she', 'he/she', '(s)he' and suchlike, I'll be glad if you'll send it on. In the meantime, please read 'he', 'him' and 'his' throughout the text as embracing both men and women. No sexism is intended – after all, despite my slightly androgynous name, I am a woman.

Chriss McCallum

1
Getting Started

BEFORE YOU STEP IN

To be a writer, all you have to do is apply your pen to paper and let the words flow out. Writing for the sheer pleasure of expressing your thoughts and feelings is a very satisfying activity.

But it isn't satisfying enough for *you*, is it? You don't just want to be a writer – you want to be a *published* writer.

There are no foolproof methods. There are no absolute rules. You can write anything you like. To get your work into print, however, there's one fact of life you can't afford to ignore: writing for publication is a hard-headed and fiercely competitive business. If you accept that at the outset, you'll approach your writing and the business of selling it in the best way and with the best chance of success.

It's a **buyer's market**. Don't underestimate what that means. The acceptance rate for unsolicited book manuscripts, for instance, is about one in two thousand – very long odds. But you *can* shorten them. You can:

- get to know how the publishing business works

- learn how to identify, analyse and approach your markets

- understand why you have to offer editors what they want, not what you think they *should* want

- learn how to develop a mutually profitable professional relationship with the editors you want to do business with.

The writing world is full of hopeful authors who will never see a word of theirs in print because they don't – or won't – understand that they have to study and work at both the craft of writing and the art of selling.

Serving your apprenticeship

There's no secret recipe, no magic formula for success. Tedious it might sound, but the only way to succeed is to work. Writing is a creative art, yes, but the art can only be developed from a sound knowledge of the craft. You would never dream, would you, of getting up on a public platform to play the piano if you didn't know one note from another? Yet legions of writers bombard editorial offices with manuscripts that are unstructured, badly written, and all too often directed to the wrong publisher anyway. These writers are constantly amazed and upset because their offerings boomerang home trailing rejection slips.

You don't have to court such disappointment. You can take the time and trouble to learn:

- the **basic techniques** of good writing

- how to **structure** your writing

- how to **choose and use language** to the best possible effect

- how to **communicate your thoughts** without muddle or ambiguity

- how to **capture and hold your reader's interest**

- how to **revise and rewrite**, and rewrite again until you're sure the work is as good as you can make it.

Throughout this book you'll find references to books and magazines, courses, associations, services and information sources that will help you master the craft of writing and develop the skills you need to succeed in getting your work published. To avoid unnecessary repetition, you'll find the full details in the appendices – names, addresses, telephone numbers, and prices and subscription/ membership rates where applicable.

You'll also read words of wisdom, encouragement, and occasionally caution, from editors and from published writers, some of whom are well established and well known. You don't have to agree with them – they don't always agree with each other – but what they have to say is well worth reading. These are people who know the business. They want to help you to know it too.

Take yourself seriously

It isn't easy to think of yourself as a serious writer when you're just starting out. You're probably worried about your chances of success, and nagged by doubts that wake you up in the small hours. Maybe you're worried because you can't make up your mind about what kind of writing is right for you. Don't worry. Most writers feel like this at first – and those who are too sure of themselves tend to trip over their own egos. Have confidence in your capacity to learn. Approach your writing from the beginning in a professional manner. After all, if you don't believe in your potential ability, how can you expect to convince others?

As I myself found, one of the biggest deterrents at the beginning of a writing career is the inability to take yourself seriously. It seems as if you are yearning after an impossible dream, seeking to enter a world inhabited by the greats. It is difficult to realise that most other writers have started with the same doubts and uncertainties.

Liz Taylor, *The Writing Business*

And be taken seriously
The first part of the book is designed to help you build your credibility. It will give you a working knowledge of the business of writing and its accepted practices and conventions, to help you avoid many of the pitfalls that commonly beset the inexperienced writer.

This knowledge will also equip you to decide more easily where you want to start, and you'll get far more out of the information in the later chapters. Even if you've already chosen your field (or if your field has chosen you, as often happens), don't dismiss the other options altogether. You might want to branch out later on.

Common sense
Many beginning writers seem to be drawn to one or the other of two extreme attitudes. First, there's the new writer who devours all the advice he can lay hands on, and who treats every word as gospel. He then gets himself into a terrible twist, endlessly trying to adapt his style, his approach, his technique, his marketing strategy, because the writers' magazine or manual he's reading this week contradicts the advice in the one he read last week. He has no faith at all in his own judgement, and gives himself no chance to develop any.

Then there's the opposite type, the beginner who refuses to consider *any* advice or help from anyone. He drives editors to distraction by disregarding even the most basic common-sense principles. He's the one who shoots off book-length stories to tiny

magazines, single poems to book publishers, erudite essays to mass-market magazines . . .
Neither of these writers uses his common sense. The result is that they create problems where none need exist.

This book aims to show you the practical common-sense ways to succeed in getting your work published. Above all, it will enable you to develop reliance on your own judgement, based on the information you'll read here and in the recommended books, and then on the experience you'll gradually acquire for yourself.

Here, then, are a few basic common-sense Dos and Don'ts to bear in mind as you read:

1. *Do* study the techniques of good, clear writing, but *don't* submerge your individuality.

2. *Do* study your markets to make sure the material you send them is suitable, but *don't* carbon-copy their style and content so closely that you sacrifice every trace of originality.

3. *Do* be courteous and businesslike in all your dealings with editors, but *don't* regard them either as enemies or gods. They're not 'anti' new writers, or unapproachable, or infallible, or exalted – they're human beings with problems and prejudices, mortgages and falling hair, just like the rest of us.

4. *Do* work at cultivating your own judgement, but *don't* attempt to defy the conventions before you understand them.

5. And, above all, *do* write. *Don't* just think or talk or read or dream about writing. *Do it.*

GETTING UNDER WAY

In theory, all you need is a pen and a pad of paper. In practice, it isn't that simple. Editors won't read handwritten scripts. You need to be able to present your work in the form of a **typescript**. Though it looks like a contradiction in terms, this is usually called a **manuscript** (abbreviation 'ms', plural 'mss').

You'll save a lot of money if you type your ms yourself. Current rates for a professionally typed ms are upwards of £3 per 1,000 words plus extra for copies (and you need at least one complete copy). Even a short novel of, say, 60,000 words would cost about

£200 just for typing, more than the price of a good electronic typewriter. Add a few short stories and you might as well buy a word processor. Keyboard skills are not difficult to learn. There are short courses and evening classes, or you could follow a home study course like Brenda Beaver's *Learn to Type in Thirty Days.*

SELECTING BASIC EQUIPMENT

You need pens, and small notebooks you can carry in your pocket or bag, to note *anything* that might be useful. If you can afford one, a pocket tape recorder is even better. Ideas, impressions, words, phrases, overheard anecdotes – they can slip away forever if you don't note them at the time.

Students' A4 lined notepads are popular with writers who write their first drafts in longhand. Others prefer to work straight on to a keyboard. Whichever method you choose, you'll eventually need the following to market your writing:

- If you work on a word processor or computer, a decent letter-quality printer. Most editors dislike dot matrix printers. Some, especially in the USA, refuse to read work produced from them.

- Plain white A4 bond paper. (Don't waste it on notes or drafts – anything will do for those. Save unwanted flyers, defunct letters and the like.)

- Few people use carbon copies these days, and you should never send carbon copies to editors. Get clean sharp photocopies made, and keep your original mss in case you need more.

- Black ribbons. Replace the reusable kind well before they wear out. (With an electronic typewriter and a correctable ribbon you'll get a crisp even-toned type. 'Name' brand machines are very affordably priced nowadays.)

- Plain white business envelopes, 9 x 4.5 inches.

- Manilla envelopes, 9 x 6.5 inches, to hold A4 sheets folded once.

- A4 manilla envelopes, to send mss of more than five or six sheets without folding.

Office supply shops and mail order stationery suppliers are cheaper than high street shops for paper and envelopes. Shop around and compare prices. A4 plain white copier paper is perfectly acceptable for mss, but it doesn't erase as well as bond. Ask for 80 gsm (grammes per square metre) weight plain copier paper – it's half the price of bond. Make friends with your local office supplier. He might agree to a small discount if you undertake to buy all your stationery supplies there.

Superstores like Office World and Staples offer competitive prices and home delivery on orders over a stipulated value. Viking Direct has regular bargain offers. Find them in *Yellow Pages*.

Do you need a word processor or computer?

You can get your writing career off the ground with clean error-free typewritten mss, but more and more publishers are now asking for work to be supplied on disk as well as on paper. If you can't do this you could lose commissions. A good word processor now costs about the same as a typewriter did a few years ago, and computers, too, are getting cheaper.

Most stores have demonstration models you can try, and once you've seen for yourself the savings in time and effort word processing offers you'll wonder why you hesitated.

Remember, though, the word processor is only a tool. It can't create publishable work by magic – only you, the writer, can do the creating.

Every successful writer works in his or her own way. Fay Weldon, interviewed on Channel 4, declared that if the day ever comes when she's required to write on a machine she'll stop writing. She writes with a pen and pad, and pays someone else to type her mss. That's fine, if you can afford the luxury.

If you need help to master your new computer, look for the appropriate book in the 'for Dummies' series: *Macs for Dummies*, *DOS for Dummies*, *Windows for Dummies* and so on. They cut right through the mystique.

SELECTING USEFUL BOOKS

Buy these books if you can – you'll use them a lot.

- A big fat dictionary. *Chambers Dictionary* is excellent.

- A *current* copy of the *Writers' & Artists' Yearbook* or *The Writer's*

Handbook. Buy both if you can afford to. These are annual directories of book, magazine and newspaper publishers and what they publish, plus radio, stage and TV markets. The *Yearbook* gives lots of sound advice about writing and getting published, agents, associations, services, tax liabilities, rights, copyright and so on. The *Handbook* doesn't list as many outlets as the *Yearbook* but gives more detailed information about those it does include, and covers more radio, TV and stage outlets.

• *The Oxford Dictionary for Writers and Editors.* Useful for checking difficult spellings and usage, including many proper names, capitalisation, abbreviations, foreign words and phrases.

• *Research for Writers* by Ann Hoffmann, a comprehensive reference book for finding information sources. Get the latest edition.

• A concise encyclopedia, like the annual *Pears Cyclopedia.*

• *Roget's Thesaurus*, which lists synonyms for almost every word in the English language. Marvellous for finding just the right word – but don't get addicted to it.

Books about writing
There are dozens of books to show you how to write publishable work. You'll find details of books about writing for specific fields in the appropriate sections later in the book. The books listed here are recommended especially for new writers who want to familiarise themselves with the practice and business of writing:

• *An Author's Guide to Publishing* by Michael Legat. Book publishing, contracts, presentation, author-publisher relations.

• *Writing for Pleasure and Profit* by Michael Legat. Covers many fields of writing; particularly good on novel-writing.

• *Starting to Write* by Marina and Deborah Oliver. An introduction to writing, designed for the absolute beginner.

• *The Writer's Companion* by Barry Turner. The editor of *The Writer's Handbook* gives a comprehensive overview of the publishing scene from the writer's angle.

- *The Successful Author's Handbook* by Gordon Wells. Practical, down-to-earth guide to writing for the non-fiction markets.

- *Writing Step by Step* by Jean Saunders. A clear and concise guide for beginning writers, looking at the various choices available.

FINDING WHAT YOU NEED

Library services

The public library should be able to get *any* book for you that's published in the UK and currently in print, and many that are out of print, from other libraries in your district or through the Inter-Library Loan Service, which operates through the British Lending Library. This might involve a small charge (usually under £1).

As you'll probably be using the library a good deal, it's worth making a note of the main category divisions of the Dewey Decimal Classification System, which is used in most UK libraries. The category numbers are shown on the shelves, and it saves time if you know where to start looking:

000	General Works
100	Philosophy
200	Religion
300	Social Sciences
400	Languages
500	Science
600	Technology
700	The Arts and Recreations
800	Literature
900	Geography, Biography and History.

Out-of-print books and books on your special subjects

The monthly *Book and Magazine Collector* lists books for sale and wanted, together with articles and information about collectable authors and illustrators and their works. Although it's primarily intended for book dealers and collectors, it's useful for writers, too. Many book dealers specialise, and you can ask those who specialise in your own fields of interest to put you on their mailing lists. Or you can advertise for books yourself. The magazine also carries advertisements for book-finding services, dealers who will find particular books for you through their contacts in the business.

Writers' magazines

There are magazines specially produced for writers. They print advice, news, reviews, competition notices and other information on what's happening on the writing scene, plus articles by writers discussing the craft and business of writing and getting published.

- *Writers News* dominates this area at the moment. It's a glossy A4 monthly magazine published by David St John Thomas, former owner of David & Charles Publishers. It carries information and news snippets about markets, competitions and so on, with articles and practical advice written by a team of regular contributors augmented by well-known names in the business. Subscribers also receive the bi-monthly news-stand title *Writing Magazine*.

- *Writers' Bulletin* is a markets, resources, news and information newsletter compiled, edited and published by Chriss McCallum and John Benton. The *Bulletin* is published monthly (except August and January) and all the information it carries is checked and verified with the appropriate editors/publishers.

- *Writers' Forum* magazine, now in its fifth year, has changed hands, and new owner/editor Morgan Kenney has major plans to revamp, improve and promote this quarterly publication.

- *Writers' Own Magazine* is a friendly A5 quarterly, publishing readers' articles, short stories and poetry, plus information.

- *Flair For Words* (see under Services) publishes a bi-monthly newsletter, *Flair News*, for their members. *Flair News* carries markets, articles, hints and tips, readers' letters and more.

- *The New Writer* is an amalgam of *Quartos* and *Acclaim*, publishing short stories from the Ian St James Awards, plus articles on writing, competition news and more.

- *The Author* is the official quarterly magazine of The Society of Authors. Non-members can buy it on subscription.

Finding photographs

If you need photographs to illustrate your book you'll find a list of photographic agencies and picture libraries in the *Writers' & Artists' Yearbook*.

One of the largest agencies is Popperfoto (Paul Popper Ltd) whose commercially available visual material amounts to a staggering 15,000,000 illustrations. Popperfoto lend their material worldwide, usually on a same-day basis, for reproduction purposes. It's mainly publishers who use these services, but a private individual can use them too. However, the costs are quite high, and there's a service fee payable whether you use the illustrations or not. The use of a single black and white photograph, with UK rights only, could cost upwards of £40 plus the service charge. Popperfoto always advises authors:

- not to start researching pictures till you have a publisher

- wherever possible leave the research to the publisher – they know far more about it than authors

- make sure you have it in writing that the publisher will be responsible for payments and for the safekeeping of the photos, otherwise you might be charged for any damage.

There's a comprehensive book on the subject, *Practical Picture Research* by Hilary Evans. You can buy the book direct from Mr Evans (see page 177) but as the latest edition is rather costly you'll probably want to ask for it at your public library.

Your local photographic society
There are probably members of your local photographic society who would be delighted to supply you with photographs. You could come to an arrangement about making payments if and when your material is published, and give an undertaking that the photographer's work will be credited to him.

Free photographs
Many large industrial and commercial companies will allow you to use photographs of their products and related items free of charge, provided you give the company due acknowledgement and therefore publicity. If there's a company whose products and/or services might be suitable as illustrations for your book or article, it's worth contacting their publicity officer about this.

You could also enquire at tourist information centres. Many of these will supply free slides or prints to accompany material that promotes their area.

Take your own
Many editors welcome features offered as text-plus-pictures packages. If your photos are good enough, you might find one of your shots on a magazine cover, with appropriate reward.

Modern cameras take most of the terror out of the technical aspects of picture-taking, but you might find it useful to take a short photography course to learn about composition, lighting and so on. Gordon Wells's book *Photography for Article Writers* is a useful guide to basic techniques and gives sound advice on the kind of pictures that combine well with text and help sell your work.

FINDING INSPIRATION, SUPPORT AND TUITION

Writing can be a lonely business. Some writers prefer to work alone, but others need the stimulation of company to spark off ideas and exchange thoughts and views (and complaints about editors and agents). Once you start looking for kindred spirits, you'll be surprised how many you'll find around you.

Writers' groups

There might be a writers' group already meeting in your district, or at least close enough for you to attend occasionally. Your library will have contact names and addresses.

You can get a *Directory of Writers' Circles*, compiled by Jill Dick, which lists contact names and addresses throughout the UK. Details are in the appendices under Useful Booklets in the Further Reading section.

If you can't find a group near you, why not start one yourself? A notice in your local paper (contact the editor) or pinned up in the library should turn up at least one or two fellow scribes. You can meet once or twice a month in each other's homes, or just meet occasionally but keep in touch by telephone. With enough members, you could hire a room regularly and share the cost.

Meeting other writers in a group can help in several ways. A group provides mutual support, encouragement, and comfort when it's needed. As well as discussing work and problems, you can share the cost of subscriptions to writers' magazines, and build up a library of writers' manuals and reference books. Each member can contribute magazines for market study, and you could club together to buy stationery in bulk.

Your local Arts Council office will advise about inviting guest speakers and will help you to find them. Some Regional Arts Boards have schemes to help groups pay for visiting speakers.

Postal workshops

Sometimes called 'folios', postal workshops are systems where writers circulate their work-in-progress around a limited number of other members. In turn, each member reads and comments on the other members' work, and contributes before passing the folio on to the next member. Each workshop usually concentrates on a specific genre – writing for children, novel-writing, writing for radio and so on. The system is particularly useful for writers who find it difficult to get to writing classes or meetings of writers' groups.

The Cottage Guide to Writers' Postal Workshops has full details, regularly updated, of postal workshops, folios and similar organisations. See under Further Reading.

Classes, seminars and residential courses

Most **Local Education Authority (LEA)** and **Workers' Educational Association (WEA)** syllabuses include courses on creative writing and related subjects. These are usually advertised in the local press before the start of each term, and your library should have information.

Seminars and **courses** are held all over the country and all through the year. As you become familiar with the writing world, and receive the information that comes in and with writers' magazines, you'll see a wide range of events you can take part in.

Writers who get involved in seminars and residential courses find that their enjoyment, enthusiasm and stimulation carry over into writing at home and keep them going when they might otherwise become discouraged. This inspiration is evident to the tutors as well as their students. Ted Hughes, the Poet Laureate, takes an active part in the Arvon Foundation, and is enthusiastic in his support of the courses:

> On a good course, the excitement and delight of the students has to be seen to be believed. And no one would credit the transformation it works on many of them, unless he had seen it. The whole course is designed to achieve this result, and nine times out of ten it does achieve it. The tutors want it to happen, and the students want it to happen, so it happens.
>
> Ted Hughes, the Poet Laureate

- The **Arvon Foundation** offers residential courses at its three centres, Lumb Bank in Yorkshire, Totleigh Barton in Devon and Moniack Mhor, Inverness. Five-day courses include board, lodging and tuition. Reductions are available to the low-waged, unemployed, students and pensioners. There are facilities for disabled people. The course tutors include some of the best-known writers in the country, like P D James and Stan Barstow. Write for details of current and projected courses, and prices.

- The **Writers' Summer School**, Swanwick, is a six-day annual event. This is the oldest established of the writers' conferences, having begun in 1949. There are about 350 places, but it's usually oversubscribed so you should apply early. The conference is held in August, and attracts top writers as tutors and speakers. Details and application form sent on request.

- The **Writers' Holiday in Wales** is a week-long gathering of writers held at Caerleon each summer in the last week of July. The programme includes workshops, tutorials, seminars, talks and outings, and attracts a wide mix of writers – beginners, 'up-and-comings' and the well-established. Details on request.

- The **National Institute of Adult Continuing Education (NIACE)** issues a comprehensive handbook every six months, giving the half-year's list of residential short courses held at various locations. NIACE will send you the handbook for a small charge – it lists many creative writing courses.

- **Network Scotland Limited** supplies information on creative writing courses throughout Scotland, as well as information leading to qualifications in literature and journalism. Each enquiry is dealt with as it comes, as the information available is extensive and changes frequently. You can enquire by phone or letter, or drop in personally. Network Scotland will also send you a leaflet about their **education information services**.

Contact your Regional Arts Board

Ask the office of your nearest Regional Arts Board to put your name on their regular mailing list of literary events: Writers-on-Tour, readings, workshops, information about books and other material published locally. (Local publishers are often interested in work by local writers.) You'll also receive information about **arts festivals**, where you can make contact with other writers and possibly have the opportunity to read your own work. Your library will have the address.

Correspondence courses

The value of correspondence courses is a subject of on-going, often heated, debate. One writers' magazine conducted a survey among its readers and found that success or failure appeared to depend almost entirely on the calibre of the tutors. The response from course students, past and current at the time of the survey, also indicated that the chances of a student being allocated a competent and helpful tutor are no more than 50-50. Students' comments ranged from 'my tutor was all I hoped for and more. I have recouped the cost of the course three times over' through 'kindly comments but very little constructive criticism' to 'worse than useless – some of the markets I was advised to send my work to no longer existed'.

It appears, too, that in most cases the only qualification needed to be appointed as a tutor is to be a 'published writer' – of what and how long ago doesn't seem to be an issue. Tutors are not well paid in relation to the cost of the courses, so it seems reasonable to assume that, with a few honourable exceptions, they're unable or unwilling to spend a great deal of time on each student assignment. Success would appear to be as much a matter of luck, than, as of hard work on the student's part. When you consider how much these courses cost, this is not encouraging.

The student drop-out rate is very high. According to information from several tutors, many students give up in the early stages, and a significant number do nothing at all after the first or second assignments, even if they've paid the full cost.

The bigger schools advertise widely in the national press and in consumer magazines. Smaller enterprises advertise in writers' magazines. Hold off till you get on to the information grapevine through writers' groups and magazines, and never send money before you've seen references. In a 1997 court case, a woman was jailed for six months and ordered to pay back £3,000 in compensation to 53 aspiring writers who responded to her ad for a writing course. The 'course' was three hand-written paragraphs on finding work as a writer. Be warned – always check credentials.

Your money might be better spent on building a library of good writers' manuals and on attending a few seminars or, if you can manage it, a writers' holiday. You'll get more from these 'face-to-face' meetings than from most distance-learning courses.

The Internet

Writers' conferences are already up and running on the **Internet** and the **world wide web**. If you're interested in joining in with these international discussion and help groups, you'll need a suitable computer and a modem connected to a telephone line or a cable line. There are several books available to help you demystify the technological aspects of getting 'on-line'. Here's a small selection:

- Graham Jones, *How to Use the Internet* and *Doing Business on the Internet*.

- John R Levine, Carol Baroudi & Margaret Levine Young, *The Internet for Dummies*.

- Angus J Kennedy, *The Rough Guide to the Internet & World Wide Web*.

CHECKLIST

Start drawing up a plan of action. Here are a few basic first steps – you can add to them as your knowledge grows and your ambitions begin to focus.

Objectives

1. **Begin to learn about the writing business**. Buy, or borrow from the library, *The Writer's Companion* (Barry Turner), *Writing for Pleasure and Profit* (Michael Legat), *Journalism for Beginners* (Joan Clayton).

2. **If you can't type, take action to learn**. Buy or borrow a reasonably good machine. Buy a typing manual or arrange tuition. Most local authorities run courses.

3. **Join (or initiate) a writers' group**. Make enquiries at the library. Advertise for other writers to make contact. Send for *The Cottage Guide to Postal Workshops*.

4. **Begin to learn about the pleasures and problems you'll have in common with other writers, both new and experienced**. Send for a copy of at least one writers' magazine.

5. **Start to whet your appetite for eventual publication**. Buy and read through the *Writers' & Artists' Yearbook* or *The Writer's Handbook* – both, if you can.

KEEPING RECORDS

To keep your writing affairs in order, you should start keeping simple records right at the beginning. Note everything down as it happens. (If you leave it till the end of the month – or even the end of the week – you'll probably forget something.) You need the following:

1. A **cash book**, to record expenditure. Note every penny spent, including the purchase of this book, and file the receipts. (With the advent of self-assessment for taxation, you're required by law to keep contemporaneous records of any expenses you intend to set against tax.) Note, too, any money you earn from your writing, no matter how small the sum.

2. A **record book**, to keep track of your articles, stories, poems – where you send them, whether they're accepted or rejected, paid for or not and so on.

3. A **markets book**, to record your dealings with individual markets. Keep detailed notes as you gather information and experience of each one. List every item you send there, and keep a record of its progress. Note how you found that market to deal with – friendly or offhand, prompt or slow, efficient or not... Note changes in editorial personnel, policy and so on, anything that might be useful in future dealings there (even if it's only 'Never again!').

4. A **'writing only' diary**, or a set of labelled folders, any system that suits your type of writing. You need to keep track of deadlines, seasonal material, forthcoming competitions and the like.

The cash book

Any money legitimately spent on your writing business – on equipment, stationery, stamps, books and magazines, phone calls, subscriptions, travelling expenses and so on – could be tax-deductible against future earnings, and you could be asked to produce receipts to support your claims.

By law, you must declare your earnings, however modest, in each financial year. The only exception *at the time of writing* is that competition prizes are not taxable.

199X

June		£	p
1	2 ribbons	5	76
	pkt paperclips		65
	1 ream bond paper	6	50
	(John Jotter Ltd)		
11	20 x 20p stamps	4	00
	10 x 26p stamps	2	60
14	Book: 'Starting to Write'	8	99
	(Bookbuff & Co)		
	Sub renewal (*Writers' Bulletin*)	20	00
17	Photocopying 'Bees' Article		50

199X

June		£	p
9	'Top Tip' + photo (*Chat*)	20	00
21	Article (*The Lady*)	55	00

Fig. 1. Two facing pages from a cash book.

If you spend a lot on postage – and most writers do – it's a good idea to keep a separate postage book, to log details of out-going letters and packages. Enter purchases of stamps and International Reply Coupons (IRCs) in your cash book and account for their use by logging each item posted, with destination, date of posting and so on, in your postage book. In this way, you'll have to account (to yourself) for every stamp or IRC you use, so you won't be tempted to raid your 'writing' stamps for other letters.

The usual book-keeping practice is to record debit entries (money spent) on the left-hand page and credit entries (money received) on the facing right-hand page (see Figure 1).

The record book

A loose-leaf book is best for this, so you can add pages as you need them. Keep a page for each item you write. You should be able to see at a glance what's happening to each story, article or poem (see Figure 2).

Item: Short story	*Title*: 'Alien Love'	*Length*: 1,246 words		
Date sent	Sent to	Accepted/ rejected	Payment received	Date
25.1.9X	*Bella*	Rejected	–	17.3.9X
3.4.9X	*Dreamland*	Accepted	£100	16.9.9X

Fig. 2. Page from a record book.

The markets book

Keep a page for each target market, and list every item you send to that market. This is a simple system, easy to keep up to date, and it will help you to avoid misdirected or duplicated submissions (see Figure 3).

Dreamland 11 Milky Way Starville XX7 7XX				Editor: Verity Verucca		
Date sent	Item	Accepted/ rejected	Payment received	Date	Remarks	
3.4.9X	Short story	Accepted	£100	16.9.9X		

Fig. 3. Page from a markets book.

Before putting pen to paper there are still some important matters to consider which often appear more daunting to budding writers than they need be: **copyright, plagiarism** and **libel.**

UNDERSTANDING COPYRIGHT

Copyright simply means 'the right to copy'. No one else has the right to reproduce, print, publish or sell any part of your writing without your permission. The law protects your copyright during your lifetime and for 70 years after your death. Your copyright is your property; you can sell it outright if you wish, but you would then have no further claim on that work or on any money it might make in the future.

In the UK, you don't have to register your copyright. It belongs to you the minute you set your words down on paper. (This even applies to your personal letters; the *letter* belongs to the recipient, but the *words* you wrote still belong to you, and no one has the right to publish them without your written consent.)

The copyright line you see in books and magazines – the author's name preceded by the sign © – is a warning to the public that the work is protected. There's no need to put this line on your ms – your work is already protected, and it's highly unlikely that a publisher would steal your material.

However, if you're worried about your copyright being infringed even before you see your work in print, you can protect yourself quite easily. Send a copy of your ms to yourself by registered post, then take the unopened package and your receipt (make sure the date is clear) to a safe place like a bank. Deposit them, and get a receipt there as well. You'll then have concrete proof of when your ms was written, should you ever need it.

If you're tempted to sell your copyright...

A publisher might ask you to sell your material outright, including the copyright, for a fixed one-off payment. You should avoid doing this even if the wolf has a foot and a half inside your door. You don't know what goodies you might be signing away. The publishing world is full of hard-luck stories about this. The most dramatic is the tale of an aristocratic family who fled to America when the Nazis occupied Europe. Hungry, disorientated and unsure of their future, they sold their story for the price of a few weeks' food and lodging. They signed away their copyright, and with it all future claims on the story. The family's name was Von Trapp, and their story became the multi-million-dollar musical *The Sound of Music*. The Von Trapps didn't get another cent.

The copyright laws operate both ways

Just as your work is protected from other writers' plundering, so their work is protected from you. You can't use other people's writing without their consent, meaning that you can't quote any substantial part of another writer's work without written permission. And that permission can be expensive. At the time of going to press the recommendations of the **Society of Authors** and the **Publishers' Association** for *basic minimum fees* for quotation and anthology use are:

* prose: £82 per 1,000 words
* poetry: £30 for the first 10 lines, £1.50 per line for the next 20 lines, and £1 per line thereafter.

Permission to use copyright material should be sought from the publishers of that material – fees can vary from publisher to publisher.

Moral rights

The provision of 'moral rights', that is, the rights of 'paternity' and 'integrity', was introduced in the **1988 Copyright, Designs. and Patents Act**.

The **right of paternity** is the author's right to be clearly identified as the creator of a work. The **right of integrity** is the author's right to prevent any distortion or mutilation of the work which would damage his or her reputation.

The 1988 Act requires the author to assert his or her moral rights in writing. (You'll see a notice to this effect in the prelims of many recently published books, especially novels.)

Moral rights are separate from actual copyright in a work. The 1988 Act provides for the **waiving of moral rights**, and some magazine publishers try to insist on writers waiving their moral rights on contributed material, sometimes to the extent of implying that such a waiver is a condition of acceptance. Writers are vigorously resisting this. Should you find yourself faced with this dilemma, do take legal advice.

The Society of Authors publishes a *Quick Guide to Copyright*, and useful books include *Copyright & Law for Writers* by Helen Shay and *The Writer's Rights* by Michael Legat.

'Fair dealing'

This term is used to describe the legitimate use of published material 'for purposes of criticism or review'. This is generally interpreted as meaning that you can quote a line or two to illustrate a point you want to make, *provided you give due acknowledgement of the source of the quotation.*

For example, in this book's chapter on writing articles, two short sentences are quoted from Gordon Wells's book *The Craft of Writing Articles* to reinforce a point made in that chapter. Both the author's name and the name of the book are acknowledged there. This is 'fair dealing'. On the other hand, the paragraph from Liz Taylor's book *The Writing Business*, quoted at the beginning of this book, is printed with the author's *written* permission. Liz Taylor would have had justifiable cause for complaint had her words been used in such a prominent way without her permission.

We shouldn't forget the gaffe made by Princess Michael of Kent when she wrote her book *Crowned in a Far Country*. She used large chunks of other authors' works without any acknowledgement at all, and was publicly criticised for this.

Till you're more familiar with the not too well defined legal niceties, it would be safer either to avoid quoting from other authors altogether or to seek permission for anything you want to quote. Your request for permission should normally be sent to the publisher, not directly to the author.

Co-authorship

The rule protecting copyright for a specified period after an author's death also applies to writing partnerships, such as an artist collaborating with an author to produce an illustrated book, a lyric-writer and a composer pooling their talents to write a song, two authors co-writing a book and so on. The work concerned doesn't come out of copyright and into the public domain – that is, free for anyone to use – until the full period of 70 years from the end of the calendar year in which the last surviving partner died.

Don't assume that because one half of a writing team has been dead for the statutory 70 years his or her work is automatically free of copyright protection. There was an expensive example of this trap in the 1960s (when the statutory period was 50 years) involving the partnership of Gilbert and Sullivan, who wrote the Savoy operas. Pye records made a jazz album, 'The Coolest Mikado', based on Sir Arthur Sullivan's music for *The Mikado*. Pye released the record in 1961, but were obliged to withdraw it almost immediately at a huge financial loss. (If you come across one of the copies that were sold before the ban, it's a collector's item.)

Sullivan had died in 1900, so his 50-years-after-death were long up. But W S Gilbert didn't die till 1911. The jazz arrangements were written and the recording made before Gilbert's copyright ran out, and his copyright protected Sullivan's music. Pye had infringed the joint copyright, and paid dearly for the mistake.

UNDERSTANDING PLAGIARISM

Plagiarism is the use without permission, for your own purposes, of work in which the copyright is held by someone else. There's no copyright in plots, ideas or titles, but you could have problems if, for instance, you follow someone else's storyline so closely that there's a recognisable connection.

In 1987, in America, the Estate of Margaret Mitchell brought a complaint of plagiarism against the French author Régine Desforges. Mme Desforges's novel trilogy, published in English as *The Blue Bicycle* trilogy, is clearly recognisable as a re-telling of *Gone With The Wind* in a World War Two setting. The plot and the principal characters have more than a passing resemblance to those of the famous Civil War novel. Mme Desforges did not deny that the American novel provided the inspiration for her books, but she was sued nevertheless, lost her case, and was heavily fined.

You could have problems, too, if you called your book *Catch 22* or *The Eagle has Landed*. Although there's no copyright on titles, this could be construed as a deliberate attempt to mislead.

UNDERSTANDING LIBEL

Libel is a statement made in print or writing, or broadcast in any medium, which defames the character of an identifiable living person by holding them up to hatred, contempt or ridicule.

Don't be caught out by an unintentional libel. If you make recognisable use, for instance, of a public figure (or even your next-door neighbour) as the model for a character who commits a criminal act, you could be inviting a libel suit.

The same caution applies to the use of names. If you called one of your characters David Owen, made him a GP who had once been a prominent politician, then had him commit a criminal or indecent act, the good doctor would have a pretty strong case against you.

The Society of Authors' *Quick Guides* series of booklets includes guides to copyright and libel. See under Further Reading.

2
Preparing and Submitting Your Work

WHERE WILL YOU SEND YOUR MANUSCRIPT?

You should have a clear idea of your target market *before* you begin to write an article or story. Too many new writers – and some who should know better – write the piece, revise it, polish it up and prepare the ms, *then* start looking for a suitable outlet. Successful writers seldom work that way. They write with a specific market in mind, a market they've already studied in detail. They tailor the content, treatment, style and length of the work to suit that market.

Market study is just common sense

There's no great mystique about it. Think of your writing as a product you're making for sale. No, don't frown and say you couldn't possibly think of creative writing in that way. If you want to sell your work, you *must* think like that. You're entering a business transaction, little different from selling birdseed or a three-piece suite. You are the manufacturer, and you have to supply what the retailer wants. An editor is a retailer. He buys from the manufacturer – the writer – what he knows he can sell to his customers – his readers.

The fiction editor of *Woman's Weekly* won't buy a horror story. She knows she would lose readers. Mills & Boon won't buy a science fiction novel. It's not what their customers expect from them. A literary magazine would have no slot for a DIY article. Yet misdirected mss like that boost Post Office profits year after year.

At the very least, make sure your ms is targeted at the right area of publishing, an area that publishes *that kind of material.*

SELECTING A MARKET

Start by studying the *Writers' & Artists' Yearbook* and *The Writer's Handbook*. Read right through the section you're interested in – magazines, newspapers, book publishers, radio and television outlets, theatrical producers, wherever your particular inclination lies. Don't just look up the names you know. There might be potential markets you haven't even heard of before.

Select those that seem most appropriate and take a serious analytical look at them to see what prospects they hold for you, as a new freelance writer. If guidelines are offered, send for them. These two writers' manuals, however, don't list all the possible markets. Later in the book you'll find specific sources of information about markets in the various fields. For the moment, let's look at the general principles of market study.

Shoot with a rifle – not with a shotgun

1. Make sure, *before you send anything*, that the market you have in mind is willing to consider unsolicited submissions.

2. Make sure that the content, treatment and style of your work are suitable for your target market.

3. Make sure that the length of the piece complies with the publisher's stated word limits.

Let's look at these points in detail, because if you get any of them wrong you won't only lose a possible sale, you could damage your credibility. Careless marketing warns an editor that you're not taking your business seriously.

1. Are unsolicited mss welcome?

With magazines, start with the publication itself. Look at the small print at the front or near the end. Many magazines print statements like 'No responsibility taken for unsolicited mss' indicating that such mss will at least be read, or 'No unsolicited mss' meaning that they won't. The *Writers' & Artists' Yearbook* and *The Writer's Handbook* give a good general guide to whether or not you'll be wasting your time sending unsolicited material. Some writers' publications, like *Writers' Bulletin* and *Writers News*, carry current editorial 'wants' and check them at source.

However, if you want to check the editors' willingness to at least consider your ms or your proposal, phone and ask them.

If you prefer to write, send a *brief* letter to the editorial department, addressed to the editor by name if possible. If you can't find the editor's name stick to 'Dear sir', or 'Dear madam' if it's a feminist publisher:

Dear Melissa Margin,

Do you consider unsolicited material? If you do, would you please send me any available guidelines for writers, or advise me of any subject areas not open to freelances. I enclose a stamped addressed envelope. Thank you.

Yours sincerely

Don't forget the SAE. And be patient. Publishing offices get a lot of mail, and they're chronically understaffed these days. Don't ask for free sample copies 'to study your requirements'. If it's a trade or professional publication, or one you can't find in the shops, ask if they'll send you a copy or two and invoice you for them. If they do invoice you, pay up. Your market study is your responsibility, not the publisher's. It's neither reasonable nor professional to ask another business to subsidise yours.

For books, both the *Yearbook* and the *Handbook* carry details of publishers' requirements and how they prefer to be approached.

You can get quicker answers to your questions, of course, if you ring up the editorial office. Most publishers don't mind this, so long as you don't engage them in a long conversation about your work, or generally take up a lot of time. Just ask to speak to someone in the editorial office if it's a magazine, or ask for the appropriate department if you're ringing a publishing house.

It's a good idea to prepare a short list of questions before you phone, so that you get *all* the answers you need without wasting time trying to remember them off the cuff. The kind of questions you'll probably want to ask are, for example:

1. Do you welcome unsolicited material from freelance writers?

2. Are there any subjects that are covered exclusively by your staff?

3. What lengths do you prefer?

4. Do you prefer a query first, or do you want to see the whole ms?

5. Do you have guidelines I could send for?

Note down, too, any other questions you might want to ask about a particular market. For example, if they answer 'Yes' to Question 1, and you already have a firm idea of what you would like to offer, ask for the name of the appropriate editor, so you can address your ms or your query to him or her by name. (This helps to get your correspondence on to someone's desk right away rather than have it languishing in an anonymous pile.)

Don't go into detail about what you're writing unless they ask you. Be as brief and businesslike as you can. All you need at this stage is basic information.

2. Is your material suitable?

The first and most essential point to establish is that your subject matter is acceptable and appropriate. As a beginner, you might feel most secure in this if you stick to familiar ground and write for publications you already know and like, at least till you have some experience. That old writers' adage 'write about what you know' could guide you here.

You know why *you* buy your favourite magazines, you're familiar with their tone and outlook, so you won't be likely to send them something you wouldn't want to find there yourself. You'd be pretty surprised, wouldn't you, to find a feature on building a drystone wall in *Hello!* or a piece on how to hang wallpaper in *Practical Photography*? You wouldn't be likely, then, to send such features to these publications. Yet, believe it or not, people do this kind of thing all the time.

At the very least, choose a market that's compatible with what you want to write.

Getting the tone right

The next step is to get hold of a few *recent* copies of your target magazine. (It can be worse than useless to study copies from even a few months ago, because editorial policies change frequently.) Make out a study sheet and analyse the publication, noting down all the points that strike you. Ask yourself:

1. What kind of people are likely to read this publication?
   Age range?
   Sex?
   Types of occupation?
   Their interests and hobbies?
   Their aims and ambitions?

2. Why would they want to read this particular publication?
   For pleasure and relaxation?
   For instruction?

3. Can you detect a clear editorial policy or attitude? Is the

publication delivering any kind of message to its readers?

4. What kind of topics and subjects are used?

5. Are there any topics *not* covered that you might have expected to see there?

6. What areas *appear* to be written by staff members?

The last point is one which might deceive even the most experienced writer. You'll often see market information and advice using terms like 'appears to be staff-written' or 'looks as if there would be an opening for the freelance'. You should treat this kind of advice with caution. Things are not always what they seem. In response to an enquiry from a writers' magazine, one editor remarked that a series he was running was indeed staff-written, but *only because* no freelance had ever offered him anything on that subject, and he was keen to cover it. This is one area where you can only trust 'horse's-mouth' information. Ask the editorial office.

You'll get a lot of help with your answers to the analysis questions if you study the advertisements the publication carries. They should give you strong clues about the interests, concerns and age range of its readers.

Looking at the language
Now add a section to your analysis sheet in which you look at the language that's used. The kind of questions to ask are:

1. Are the words short and simple?

2. Or more sophisticated and multi-syllable?

3. Are the sentences short and simply structured, with few subordinate clauses?

4. Or are they more complex in structure?

5. Is the general tone casual or formal?

6. Are the words, for the most part, colloquial or formal?

The advertisements can help with this too, because they build a picture in your mind of the kind of people you'll be writing for.

If you pitch the tone and language either too high or too low, you'll have less chance of producing a totally suitable piece of writing. Gordon Wells has a very detailed section on market analysis in his book *The Craft of Writing Articles*. Do read it.

3. Have you got the length right?

Most of the publications and book publishers listed in the *Writers' & Artists' Yearbook* specify the minimum and/or maximum number of words they require for each submission. There's no point in ignoring these stipulated wordage limits. Editors have a certain amount of space to fill, and they won't alter either their policy or the size of their product to accommodate a 3,000-word story if their stated limit is 2,000 words. Nor will a 50,000-word novel find a place in a list which only publishes 200,000-word blockbusters.

You'll see how to calculate your wordage in the section on preparing your mss.

Keep up to date

You're going into a business that's never static. Magazines vanish, new ones appear. Big publishers eat up little ones. Rebels set up on their own. Editors move about, and often take their pet policies and their favourite writers with them, so that their 'new' magazine might quickly become a clone of their last one.

Don't rely on last year's reference books. You could waste far more money on misdirected mss than it would cost you to replace your out-of-date information sources.

Before you send anything off, then, be sure that:

- what you're sending is suitable to the best of your judgement for the publication or publishing house you're sending it to

- you've written the piece in an appropriate style

- your ms complies with the stipulated word limits

- your target market is willing to consider it

- your market research is bang up to date.

SHOULD YOU TRY AN AGENT?

Raise the topic of agents at any writers' gathering and you can expect heated argument all round. The most common complaint heard from unpublished or little-published writers is that 'agents don't want to know you till you've already made it'.

This might be true of some agents, but it's far more likely that these disappointed writers have had their work rejected by agents for the same reason most mss are rejected by publishers. Simply, they are not good enough to publish. An agent won't take on the job of trying to place a book in which he has no confidence, any more than a publisher will accept a book he knows he won't be able to sell. A good agent chooses his clients very carefully because he'll be committing himself to a lot of work on their behalf. This is understandable when you realise that the agent won't make any money until you do, and what he eventually makes will be a percentage of what your book earns. Contrary to what some writers believe, most agents work hard for their percentages.

If an agent does take you on, you'll establish a mutually profitable working partnership. Your agent will secure better terms from publishers, and will know the home *and* overseas markets well enough to exploit the rights in your book as fully as possible. Yes, the agent gets 10 or 15 per cent of the profits – but *you* get 85 or 90 per cent, and that could mean 85 or 90 per cent of sales you wouldn't have got without the agent's know-how.

Do try to place your work with an agent if you want to, but be realistic about it. Your chances of a favourable response are about the same as your chances of acceptance by a publisher. Neither will want a substandard piece of work.

There are lists of agents in the *Writers' & Artists' Yearbook* and *The Writer's Handbook*, with details of what they handle and what they don't. Choose one who states an interest in the kind of work you've written, otherwise you'll have no chance at all. Most of the listed agents specify how they prefer to be approached – by letter, or by sending a synopsis, or by sending the full ms.

Dorothy Lumley runs the **Dorian Literary Agency**. She handles full-length fiction, specialising in women's writing, science fiction, fantasy and horror, crime and thrillers. Dorothy also takes full-length adult non-fiction. She doesn't handle short stories, poetry or children's material. Commission: UK 10 per cent, US 15 per cent, translations 20–25 per cent, performance rights 10 per cent. There is no reading fee. Dorothy prefers a first contact by letter, with sample material. Return postage is essential.

When contacting an agent please give as much information as possible, ie whether you already have one and wish to change, a CV of your published works to date, and what you want to write in future. An editor only wants to let an ms speak for itself, an agent wants to know how you view your writing career. If you received any comments on a current ms from an editor who has rejected it, it's useful to pass these on to any agent you approach.

Dorothy Lumley

Now that so many publications will not consider unsolicited short stories, preferring to buy through agencies which sift out the all-too-prevalent unsuitable and unpublishable submissions, it could pay you to let a specialist agency consider your work.

The partnership of Cari Crook and Lesley Gleeson runs **Midland Exposure**, an agency specialising in selling short stories to magazines. Cari and Lesley assess each story on its merit, and if they find material they consider well written and suitable, they will offer it to an appropriate outlet. They are working writers themselves and, sympathetic to the difficulties and frustrations of the job, offer advice, editing and encouragement to writers whose work is 'nearly there'. They charge 15 per cent commission on sales only.

The *Writers' & Artists' Yearbook* and *The Writer's Handbook* both list agents, giving details of their fields of interest. The Society of Authors publishes a *Quick Guide to Literary Agents*.

LOOKING AT OVERSEAS MARKETS

The whole English-speaking world is open to you, and some of the overseas markets are listed in the *Writers' & Artists' Yearbook*.

The USA

The biggest and most lucrative market is the United States of America. The potential for sales is enormous and many British writers have already achieved considerable success there. For the American markets, however, the marketing strategy is more clearly defined than in the UK. Almost invariably, you *must* send a **query letter** or a **proposal** first, not a complete ms. 'Over the transom' (unsolicited) submissions are vigorously discouraged. Many publishers won't even open the package – they simply mark them *'Return to sender'*.

Writers' guidelines
Before you send anything, even a query letter, you should first write to your target markets and ask for their **writers' guidelines**. Most US magazines issue these as standard practice. It's essential to enclose

International Reply Coupons (IRCs). These guidelines are usually very comprehensive and are designed to save time and expense for both the magazine and its would-be contributors. They describe the publication's requirements in detail, telling you what the editors want and how they want you to send it.

Writer's Market
You'll find around 4,000 US markets listed in the annual *Writer's Market*, a hardback book of more than 1,000 pages which also includes articles and tips on freelance writing. The market information is comprehensive and detailed, and leaves little room for doubt about whether a market will suit your material and vice versa.

Writer's Market is published by Writer's Digest Books, and is stocked in the UK by major bookshops like Waterstones and Dillons. You might find a copy on the shelves in the 'Creative Writing' section, or they will order it for you.

Writer's Digest magazine, published by the same company as *Writer's Market*, is a monthly magazine carrying articles, advice and markets for the freelance writer. You can subscribe direct, and the magazine usually offers preferential terms for new subscribers. Write for information, enclosing an IRC.

American Markets Newsletter
Edited and published by Sheila O'Connor, this monthly newsletter lists American markets ranging from mainstream USA-wide publications to specialist, local and literary magazines and book publishers, many of them not listed in *Writer's Market*. Worth a subscription if you seriously want to break into the US market.

Tips on writing for American magazines
1.   Always send for guidelines first.

2.   At the same time, ask for a copy of the magazine, enclosing IRCs to pay for it and for return postage. Many of the magazines listed in *Writer's Market* specify how many IRCs you should send.

3.   Study the sample magazine carefully for style.

4.   Invest in an American-English dictionary – many spellings and meanings are different, and it's essential that you write your

material in 'American' English. You're a pro, remember.

5. Offer 'First North American Rights'.

6. For mss, use paper cut to US standard size: 8.5 x 11 inches.

WRITING SEASONAL AND ANNIVERSARY MATERIAL

Seasonal material

'**Seasonal material**' describes writing whose subject matter relates to a particular season of the year: Christmas, Easter, Hallowe'en and so on.

Seasonal material must be sent well in advance, anything from three months to a year or even more. It's no use waiting until October to submit a Christmas story to a magazine – the Christmas issue will be ready to print by then.

You need to check your target publications' seasonal deadlines. Phone the editorial department and ask. No one will mind, provided you're brief and businesslike.

Insider tip 1
Write your seasonal pieces *during the season*. It's hard to get into a 'mistletoe-and-holly' mood when you're drooping over a hot sticky keyboard on a sweltering summer's day. File the piece away, and make a note to remind you when to send it off. Get it out a few days early and give it an objective critical reading. You might see faults you didn't notice when you wrote it, and you'll have time to put them right and to give the work the final polish that can make the difference between a sale and a rejection.

Insider tip 2
Avoid including any reference to current events, unless your piece is intended to be relevant to that year only. Topical references will make it unsaleable in future years.

Anniversary material

'**Anniversary material**' describes writing whose theme is a past event, intended for publication on or near an anniversary of that event. Like seasonal material, anniversary pieces must be submitted well in advance, especially if the event being commemorated is well known and widely documented.

As a beginner you would probably be wasting your time writing about, for instance, D-Day or a Royal birthday, unless you've unearthed something new and/or sensational. You could try sending a query letter, but it's likely that your target market already has material on the subject either in stock or commissioned from a regular contributor or from a famous 'name'.

The Writers' & Artists' Yearbook prints a useful Journalists' Calendar of up-coming anniversaries.

Your local papers and magazines might welcome features about the anniversaries of interesting local people and events, especially if you can link them to something that's happening today. Working from local knowledge, you can start researching early enough to offer the editor a feature packed with facts and human interest – and that's the kind that sells.

PREPARING YOUR MANUSCRIPT

There's a standard layout you should always follow when you're typing short stories, articles or books. (Poetry, playscript and picture-script layouts are shown in the relevant chapters later.) A well presented ms could increase your chances of acceptance. A slovenly one could destroy them.

First impressions count

Your ms says a lot about *you*. Give an editor a crisp, clean, well set out ms, with accurate spelling, grammar and punctuation, and you give him a degree of confidence in its content, even before he reads it. You've shown him you care about what you're doing, and that you're approaching the job in a professional way. Even if he doesn't want *this* piece, you'll have banked some goodwill for the future.

A sloppy ms won't get a warm welcome. Don't imagine that the editor will toil manfully through a scruffy script, ignoring coffee stains, over-typings, blisters of Tipp-Ex, your bald ribbon or your ink-starved dot matrix printer, in a tireless quest for literary genius. He won't. He might not bother to read it at all, because he'll judge, probably accurately, that you won't handle *any* of your business efficiently.

You're offering your work for sale in a highly competitive market. Don't turn your customers off with tatty packaging.

Don't rush it. When you've done a complete draft:

• Check your spelling, grammar, punctuation and syntax.

- Alter any clumsy phrasing or repetitions.

- Check that all personal and place names are accurate and consistent. Page one's brown-eyed Babs mustn't have blue eyes on page five, so check your descriptions for consistency, too.

- Check *any* facts you're not absolutely sure about. If an editor spots the smallest inaccuracy of fact, he'll start to worry that there might be a big one somewhere.

- *Insider tip*: When you've read each page for its sense, read it again line by line *from the bottom up*, covering the lines below as you go. This is a proofreader's trick that throws up misspellings you might easily miss in a straight reading.

- Finally, check the word count – see below. As you've seen when you read about market study, you should be working with a particular market in mind. Check *now* whether you need to cut any excess wordage.

Calculating your wordage
For a magazine article or short story, you should count every word and put the total word count, rounded up to the nearest ten, on your ms. Little space is wasted in magazines because of the narrow column widths.

Books are different. Look at the text of any conventional book. You'll see that while most of the lines occupy the full width of the text, many do not. Take, for example, lines like:

> She looked up.
> 'Oh no,' she sighed.
> 'It's true.'

Here you have just nine words – and they use up three lines.

You can see, then, what a distorted picture you'll get if you simply count words. You should treat *every* line, however short, as a full line, including the last lines of paragraphs. Think of the whole text area as being solid with words.

This is how to do it:

1. Count the exact number of words in five sets of ten full lines picked at random through the text. Add these five sets of

numbers. Divide the total by 50. This gives the average number of words per line.

2. Add up the total number of lines in your ms, counting every line as a full line. With a reasonably consistent number of lines per page, you can multiply the total number of pages by the average number of lines per page.

3. Multiply the total number of lines by the average number of words per line.

Here's an example:

Total number of words in 50 full lines	=	710
Average number of words per line = 710/50	=	14.2
Total number of pages in the ms	=	193
Average number of lines per page	=	28
Total number of lines in the ms = 193 x 28	=	5,404
Total number of words = 5,404 x 14.2	=	76,736.8

Round this figure *up* to the nearest thousand, so your final word count, the one you would type on your ms, would be 'About 77,000 words'.

Make it beautiful
Use good quality plain **white A4 bond paper**. It will have to stand up to a lot of handling and editorial marking if your ms is accepted. If you're working on a typewriter, send a good clear photocopy and keep your original for making further copies if they're needed. Never send carbon copies to an editor.

Whatever you're working on, make sure your ribbon or printer is good enough to produce a clear, sharp, black, **easy-to-read type**. Use only a black ribbon or toner, and avoid fancy typefaces and fonts (Gothic, italic, script and so on). And however keen you are to save paper, *never* use a condensed type. Keep the typeface as plain and easy on the eye as possible. Don't send uncut continuous print-out sheets – cut and trim them.

Leave **good margins** all round, at least an inch, with a bit more on the left, where space will be needed for typesetting instructions. Keep your pages uniform in layout.

Type in **double spacing**. That means leaving one *full* line of blank space between the lines of type. It *does not mean* leaving a half line of space, and it *does not mean* hitting the space bar twice between words.

Even if your machine has the facility to do so, **don't justify** (make even) the right-hand margin. This complicates length calculations. Don't leave extra space between paragraphs, either, but do indent the first line of each paragraph so it's absolutely clear where the paragraphs begin and end.

Don't underline anything unless you intend it to appear in italics.

Identify your work

Put your name and address on your cover sheet and on the first and last pages of text. Number the pages consecutively, even for a full-length work – don't begin again with 'Page one' at the start of each chapter.

At the top right of each page, type your name, the title (or an abbreviation of it) and the page number. This is called a **strap-line**, and it ensures that your pages don't get out of order (or mislaid).

At the bottom right of every page except the very last, type '**mf**', which means 'more follows', telling the editor and the typesetter there's more copy to come. Under the last line of the last page, type 'ends'.

Follow the layout as shown in Figure 5.

Good reasons for following conventional layouts

It really *is* essential to stick to the conventional forms of manuscript layout. These haven't come about by chance, or been chosen at random. They're the layouts publishers and printers have found to be the clearest, quickest, safest and least expensive to work on:

- **Clearest** because the double-spaced lines of plain black type on white paper are easy to read and least tiring to copy editors' and typesetters' eyes.

- **Quickest** because the good margins and double-spaced text leave enough room for editorial corrections and typesetting instructions to be marked clearly and rapidly, and also because they speed length calculations.

- **Safest** because their clarity reduces the risk of typesetting errors or misunderstandings, even after corrections have been marked.

- **Least expensive** because all the foregoing points contribute to speed and accuracy, cutting the time-schedules and reducing the need for costly corrections at proof stage – and so keeping costs down and quality high.

About 1,000 words

21 Our Street
Printville
England PS99 0XX

The Christmas Kitten

by

Patricia Brennan

FSBR

Fig. 4. Example of a cover sheet.

Your observation of the preferred layouts will contribute substantially to your professional credibility.

The cover sheet
The cover sheet for the story in Figure 5 would look something like that shown in Figure 4. The layout can be varied, but the important thing is to show all the necessary information.

FBSR
The abbreviation **FBSR** stands for **First British Serial Rights**, and means that you're offering the right to publish your article or story for the first time in the UK. You can only offer this right if the piece hasn't been published in the UK before – if it has, you should give the editor its publishing history in your covering letter, and offer second rights.
The term FBSR is not used for full-length book mss.

The final check
Before you pack up your work for posting, give it a final read through. Make any necessary corrections as neatly and clearly as you can. Retype any heavily corrected pages.

DEALING WITH ILLUSTRATIONS

Some magazines, especially the heavily illustrated kind, won't consider articles without illustrations. You should find out what kind of illustrations are preferred before you send anything. Black and white prints should be glossy – they give sharper reproduction than matt-finish ones. Colour pictures are submitted either as prints, packed between sheets of stiff card, or as transparencies, which should be protected by plastic mounts (never glass).

If your work requires diagrams, maps, line drawings and so on, it should be enough to send roughs in the first instance, or photocopies of artwork if you can supply it yourself.

Don't stick illustrations on to the ms. Pencil *very lightly* an identification number on the back of each one, and pencil the numbers in the ms margins where you would like them to go. The page layouts might not allow illustrations to be placed exactly where you indicate, but they'll be placed as near as possible. Type captions on a separate sheet and number them to correspond with the numbers on the illustrations.

1,000 words

Patricia Brennan
21 Our Street
Printville
England PS99 0XX

The Christmas Kitten

by Patricia Brennan

It was nearly Christmas. There was snow on the ground and it felt very cold.

A little black kitten was out all on its own. 'Miaow,' he said. 'My paws are cold and my ears are cold and all of me is cold. Oh, I do wish I had not got lost.' But there was no one to hear the little black kitten.

He ran along a path and felt a bit warmer then. Suddenly he saw some light from a house in front of him.

'Perhaps the people there would like a kitten to live with them,' he thought, so he went towards the light. When he reached the house, he saw that the light was coming from a back door which was open. The little black kitten ran inside the house. It was warm in there and he felt so pleased that he had found this lovely house.

Suddenly there was a loud bark and a large dog charged into the kitchen. 'What are you doing here?' he said. 'Don't you know this is my house? You can't share my food. Go away with you.'

'But I am so cold and hungry,' said the kitten. 'Can I not stay with you? I won't eat much and I do need a home.'

'No, you can't,' said the dog. 'This is my home and I am not having any other animals here with me. Be off with you.'

The little black kitten went out again into the cold, dark

mf

Fig. 5. How to lay out a page.

PEN-NAMES

You can use a pen-name if you want to. This should be shown in the
byline, but *not* above your address. For instance, if Patricia Brennan
had wanted *The Christmas Kitten* to appear under the name of, say,
Alice Brent, she would have typed her own name and address as
shown, but under the title of the story, on both the cover sheet and
the first page of text, she would have typed 'by Alice Brent'.

APPROACHING AN EDITOR

Before we look at the best (and worst) ways of making your first
contact, you can be reassured about one thing: no editor will turn
down a good piece of work solely because you didn't get your
approach exactly right first time.

Provided you communicate in a courteous, businesslike way, the
editor will either consider your submitted ms anyway, or return it
and advise you about the preferred approach.

Find out what to do
It does smooth the way all round, though, if you find out and follow
each editor's preference. You can do this by:

- looking up the publication or publishing house in the *Writers' &
  Artists' Yearbook* or *The Writer's Handbook*, where the entry
  should at least give you a clue

- or phoning a brief enquiry to the editorial office, asking:
  1. 'Do you prefer to see a letter, a synopsis, or the complete script
  in the first instance?'
  2. 'What is the name of the editor to whom I should address my
  submission?' You might be offered some other useful information
  at this point, too – for instance, that the editor in question is on
  holiday for a month, or that there's already a large backlog of
  unsolicited mss waiting to be looked at.

If you can't get hold of any specific information – maybe a phone
call over a long distance in peak hours would be too expensive for
you – then, in general, it's best to:

- approach a book publisher by letter, enclosing a synopsis

- send the complete ms of a short story, whatever the length
- send the complete ms of a very short article (500 words or less)
- send a letter of enquiry about an article of more than 500 words.

(See also Chapter 5 for letters of enquiry about articles, and Chapter 6 for details of how to market non-fiction books.)

One professional to another

Every detail of your approach should be designed to give a positive impression of your professionalism. Here's how to do that:

1. Do enclose a **covering letter**. You want to establish contact with the editor, without appearing either pushy or distant. Your covering letter acts as an introductory handshake. Covering letters and letters of enquiry should be typed as normal business letters, single spaced, not double spaced like mss.

2. Do keep your letter **brief and to the point**. It shouldn't be necessary to tell the editor what your enclosed ms is all about, or to explain the point of your short story – that should be evident from the ms itself or from your synopsis. (A letter of enquiry sent by itself, of course, needs more detail.)

3. Do find out the **name of the appropriate editor** if you possibly can. Many magazines list the various editorial functions, or you can ring the switchboard and ask for the name you need. Failing all else, then 'Dear Editor' is acceptable – just. It's certainly better than 'To whom it may concern' or anything like that.

4. Do enclose an **SAE** big enough and bearing adequate postage for the return of your work. This is a convention that writers ignore at the risk of never hearing of their ms again. Every publishing office has at least one drawer full of unsolicited mss sent without either a return envelope or postage. The editor didn't invite them, so why do these writers expect him to stand the cost of returning them? Small magazines in particular just can't afford to pay for stationery and stamps to return unsolicited material.

Mervyn Fullohope
5 Colophon Cottages
Upper Case
Brighton BN99 9XYZ
Tel. (01234) 56789

21 April 199X

Melissa Margin
Fiction Editor
Rosy Dreams Magazine
Queen's Folly Buildings
London E1 1OH

Dear Melissa Margin,

Will you please consider the enclosed short story for publication in 'Rosy Dreams' at your usual rates.

The story 'And the Stars were Shining' is 3,220 words long.

I enclose the customary stamped addressed envelope.

Yours sincerely

Mervyn Fullohope

Fig. 6. How to write a covering letter.

6 Nether Avenue
Satchelmouth
Lincoln

Macdonald Mentor
Editor in Chief
The Southeastern Articulator
London

Dear Mac

I'm enclosing a batch – ten or so – of my short stories. I hope you'll like at least a few well enough to publish them – and pay.

My friends think my stories are a lot better than most of the stuff that's getting published. What do you think? By the way, I've tried one or two other mags, but the editors were stocked up, they said. None of the stories have been published before, so you can have first choice.

I know I'm supposed to enclose a stamped addressed envelope, but you don't have to send these copies back – just let me know what you decide, one way or the other. I'd be very grateful, too, if you could give me a few comments about the stories. Any advice at all would be welcome. Please don't give me the usual 'The editor regrets' brush-off. It's so discouraging. Sometimes I think editors just don't give a damn about a writer's feelings. I'm sure you're not like that, Mac. A few tips on where else I could try them would be useful, too, just in case you don't use short stories (I haven't actually seen your magazine – or is it a newspaper? – but I've seen it mentioned a few times somewhere).

Anyway, thanks for your time, and all the best!

Barney Blunder, hopeful writer.

Fig. 7. How not to write a covering letter.

And how not to do it

1. Don't send a covering letter that will take the editor as long to read as your ms would, telling him the history of your life and your writing career and assuring him that your family, friends and writers' group consider you a genius.

2. Don't embarrass the editor with emotional blackmail. His heart will sink and his hackles will rise as he reads that you're unemployed and need the money to feed your children, that you're 99 and unlikely to survive beyond his next issue, or that your doctor has prescribed creative writing as therapy following your nervous breakdown and of course any suggestion of a rejection might tip you over the edge again. (Yes, people do these things.)

3. Don't be grovelling, condescending or demanding – just be businesslike. Any other approach will raise doubts about your professionalism, and by implication about whether you'll be reliable and reasonable to work with in the future.

4. Don't send any piece to more than one magazine at a time – editors won't look kindly on a writer with a reputation for doing this. (You *can* send the same proposal to more than one book publisher at the same time. This is accepted practice now.)

5. Don't use umpteen-times recycled envelopes. We all like to save trees, not to mention money, but keep the economy labels and impenetrable layers of sticky tape for your private letters. Economies like this in business correspondence are counter-productive. They project entirely the wrong image, that of the amateur 'scribbler'. And don't send an SAE so decrepit that the editor will cringe and wonder how often it's been licked before. William Brohaugh, former editor of *Writer's Digest* magazine, says in his book *Professional Etiquette for Writers* that using recycled envelopes to present your ms is like 'wearing a rumpled suit to a job interview'.

6. Don't either, use your day-job company's letterheaded paper, or send your ms in envelopes bearing the company logo and franked at its expense. This practice has the taint of petty stinginess, and does not inspire confidence.

CHECKLIST

Check these before you make your first contact with an editor:

1. You're contacting an appropriate outlet.

2. You've ascertained as far as you can that you're following the publisher's preferred method of approach.

3. You've checked on the name of the appropriate editor.

4. Your covering letter/letter of enquiry is businesslike and totally to the point, and you haven't brought in any irrelevancies.

5. You've enclosed a suitable SAE with your story or article, or enough return postage with your full-length ms.

6. Your stationery is crisp and clean, as is appropriate to your professionalism.

Insider tip

Phrase your letter carefully, and try to assess the effect your words will have on the editor who reads them. For instance, the following sentences are guaranteed to trigger editorial alarms:

- 'Here is a short story that is a good deal better than those you've been publishing lately . . .'

- 'I am 16, and have decided to make writing my career . . .'

- 'A rejection won't discourage me. It's my life's ambition to get my work published in your magazine, so I'll keep trying till I succeed . . .'

- 'You will appreciate that I am a beginner, which is why I'm sending my work to you before I try to get published in something more literary . . .'

- 'Caution: This story is copyright, and I have taken the precaution of lodging a dated copy with my solicitor . . .'

FOLLOWING UP YOUR SUBMISSION

If you don't get a response within a reasonable time, say eight or ten weeks, contact the company and enquire about your ms, either by letter or telephone. If this gets no response either, you'll have to decide whether to try placing your work elsewhere or whether you're so keen on that market that you're prepared to give them more time. These days, magazines and publishing houses have cut staffing levels so near to the bone there's usually a backlog of mss.

However, courtesy should work both ways. If you feel you're being dealt with unfairly, write to the editor stating that your submitted work is no longer on offer and that you're sending it elsewhere. Keep a copy of the letter. (You did keep a copy of the work, didn't you?)

COPING WITH REJECTION

Rejection – a dismal word for a depressing event: an editor has refused your brain-child. But don't equate rejection with dejection. It happens to (almost) every writer. Hardly surprising, with hundreds of mss jostling for every opening.

The best coping strategy is to build up a regular output. Always have work in hand as well as out on offer. Don't invest all your dreams in one ms. If you're writing novels, start the next one as soon as, or even before, you've sent out your work.

And if your ms does thud back on to your doormat, *please* don't:

- tear it up and throw it away

- iron it and send it straight out again

- write an indignant letter to the editor, questioning his decision, his brains and his origins

- spread jam on his rejection slip and post it back.

What to do

Instead, take constructive action. Try to analyse what went wrong. Get some practice in developing your most precious asset as a writer – the ability to make an objective criticism of your own work. Ask yourself the questions in the following checklist – and be honest, for if you refuse to face the truth you're only fooling yourself.

If you answer 'Not sure' or 'No' to any of these questions, then you've been less than totally professional in your approach. It doesn't pay to skimp the hard work.

CHECKLIST

	Yes	Not sure	No
1. Are you sure the work is as good in *every way* as you could possibly make it?	☐	☐	☐
2. Did you check the accuracy of every fact and reference?	☐	☐	☐
3. Are you sure you sent the work to an appropriate market?	☐	☐	☐
4. Did you check *for yourself* that your target market is currently willing to look at unsolicited mss?	☐	☐	☐
5. Did you check *for yourself* that the slot you aimed at is not usually or exclusively written by staff or by commissioned writers?	☐	☐	☐
6. Did you study your market thoroughly?	☐	☐	☐
7. Did you tailor the work to suite the style, tone, language and length of your market?	☐	☐	☐
8. Did you check your spelling, grammar, punctuation and syntax?	☐	☐	☐
9. Did you indicate the word count?	☐	☐	☐
10. Did you present an ms that is clean, clear, neat, typed on plain white A4 paper, double-spaced, on one side of the paper only, with decent margins?	☐	☐	☐

What if your answers are all 'Yes'?

Then possibly your work has been rejected for one or more of the following reasons:

* However wonderful you, your best friend, or your writers' group tell you it is, your work is not up to publishable standards. That

means you probably haven't researched, organised or written well enough – or maybe it's just plain dull. Sorry to be blunt, but about 90 per cent of unsolicited mss fail for these reasons.

- The publisher already has a stock of this kind of material. Yours would have to be sensational to be bought at this time. You're out of luck with your timing – a hazard of freelancing.

- The editor has recently bought/commissioned/published something very similar. He might tell you this. The first two are simple misfortunes. The third would indicate that your market research hasn't been as thorough as you thought.

- The editor didn't like what you sent him. If he doesn't bother to tell you this, you'll never know. Another editor might love it.

Two questions
New writers often ask:

Do editors really read every ms they receive?

The answer to that is 'Yes'. And 'No'. Yes, they do look at every ms that comes in – no one would consciously risk missing a gem, so everything is looked at. But no, they don't read every ms right through to the end. They don't need to. An experienced editor or publisher's reader can tell from a rapid scan whether a submission is of potential value *to him*. If he doesn't think it is, he won't waste time reading it right through.

It's pointless to get up to the tricks some writers try to catch out a 'lazy' or 'prejudiced' editor. So forget about the hair or the spot of glue between the pages. They prove nothing.

Why don't editors tell me where I'm going wrong? Rejection slips are no help at all, so why don't they give me the advice I ask for?

Very few editors offer advice to writers. Writers, especially novices, tend to think this is unfair. However, there are good reasons:

- Lack of time is one. An editorial office might receive upwards of 20 or so mss every day. *Bella*, for example, receives about 700 unsolicited short stories every month in addition to those sent by agents. Even a few minutes giving constructive advice on each would take up an editor's working day – and it isn't his job.

- As explained above, an editor doesn't need to read the whole script to know if it interests him or not. He certainly doesn't need to give it a thorough critical appraisal. And advice based on less than a complete critical reading might do more harm than good. You wouldn't be getting a fair criticism at all.

- An editor's job is to find material that's suitable for his publication. It is not his job to give writing tutorials. The writing is *your* job. If you send something that is *almost* right, the editor will probably give you a few pointers and might ask you to do a rewrite 'on spec'. But when you submit an unsolicited ms, remember you're offering goods for sale in a commercial marketplace. If you were selling lampshades, you wouldn't ask your customers to show you how to make them, would you?

How books are dealt with

Most book publishers employ freelance readers to assess and report on unsolicited mss. These readers are usually experts in their field – experienced editors, authors and academics – and it's on their recommendation that an ms is either rejected outright or passed on to a second reader or an in-house editorial team.

A publisher's reader has no authority to accept a book, but his decision to reject one is seldom questioned. The acceptance rate for unsolicited book mss is very low. One publisher's reader says he's only seen two out of the 5,000 or so books he's assessed actually get into print. (This is not the glamorous job many people think it is.)

Do keep a sense of proportion, then, if the first publisher on your list rejects your first novel. You're certainly not alone.

If you must let off steam . . .

Write a nasty letter to the rejecting editor if you wish – but DON'T POST IT. Such a response would not be forgotten, and could prejudice your future chances.

The following 'rejections of rejections' are not recommended either:

- 'Please read this again. I feel sure you must have missed the whole point of the story . . .'

- 'It was with considerable amazement that I received my returned manuscript this morning. I would have thought that the least you could do was to tell me what you thought was wrong with it. Here is another story. Kindly let me have a swift response to this one, with full details of your reasons should you reject this one as well...'

- 'How could you! Your rejection has cut me to the quick! I may never have the confidence to write another word....'

- 'You just don't have the guts to give an original talent a chance...'

- 'I am returning your rejection slip herewith. I regret that it is not suited to my requirements at present...'

Persistence pays, though
Thriller writer John Creasey earned 774 rejections before he made his first sale, and Enid Blyton collected 500.

3
Self-Financed Publishing

IS IT FOR YOU?

It happens occasionally that a publisher lets a potential bestseller slip through his net (*The Day of the Jackal* is often cited as an example). However, publishers don't get it wrong as often as frustrated writers would like to believe. Many, many books are rejected because they're not remotely up to publishable standards. Many others are turned down simply because there is no ready market for them.

As a general rule, a publisher accepts a book and finances its publication because *in his judgement* it will enhance his profits or his prestige – preferably both. If your offering is rejected by publisher after publisher, but you are still convinced of its merit (or perhaps you relish the challenge of going it alone) there's nothing to prevent you publishing it at your own expense – and your own risk. Provided, that is, you understand just what you're taking on.

Do take a very careful look at what's involved. If you get carried away on a cloud of 'publication at any price' euphoria, you could be in for problems.

CHECKLIST

Is self publishing a real option for you? Before you make any commitment, ask yourself these questions:

	Yes	No
1. Do you have the necessary capital to fund the venture? It will cost upwards of £2,000 or so to typeset, print and bind a few hundred copies of a very modest book. Don't offset sales against this – there might not be any.	☐	☐

2. Have you assessed the competition? Are there
    books already published on your subject? Will
    your book be better?   ☐   ☐

3. Have you identified potential sales outlets? (Don't
    include family and friends who swear to buy a
    copy – they'll probably expect a freebie.) Is there
    really a market for what you want to sell?   ☐   ☐

4. Can you afford to lose this money if it all goes
    wrong? Be realistic, because any such venture has
    an inbuilt risk factor.   ☐   ☐

5. Do you know how to prepare the copy yourself
    (or are you willing to learn) so you can give the
    typesetter quality copy to work from? If not,
    you'll have to add these services – editing, typing,
    checking for errors, correcting the proofs – to
    your costs.   ☐   ☐

6. Do you have the time, energy and stamina to go
    out and sell your product? Or can you afford the
    services of a representative if you want to sell
    through bookshops?   ☐   ☐

If you've answered 'No' to *any* of these, perhaps you should think
again.

WHAT A REPUTABLE PUBLISHER DOES FOR YOU

When a reputable commercial publisher accepts a book for
publication, he will:

- enter into a legal contract with you, agreeing the terms under
  which he will publish your book, and giving full details of all
  rights and royalties agreed

- possibly (but not invariably) pay you a lump sum in advance
  against the royalties you'll eventually earn from the book

- arrange all the editing, designing, printing and binding

- arrange all the advertising, promotion, sales and distribution

- handle all the accounting work

- bear the cost of all the above.

He'll do all these things to the best of his ability because *his* money and *his* reputation are at stake.

You can see, then, how important it is to know what you'll be taking on. You won't have all this experience, expertise, organisation and finance behind you. You'll be on your own, and you'll be taking all the risks.

Still interested? Then let's get the biggest risk of all out of the way, so you have a fair chance of getting what you pay for.

BEWARE THE 'VANITY' PUBLISHER

He's easy to recognise. 'Authors! Does your book deserve to be published? Write to us...' he sings from the small ads in the national press. 'Publisher seeks manuscripts...', 'Let us publish your poetry...'.

What a tempting siren song it is, especially if you're smarting from yet another rejection. But...

Reputable publishers do not advertise for manuscripts

Why should they? They're knee-deep already. They can pick and choose. And they choose very carefully, because, as you've just seen, they're risking their money and reputation on their choice.

The vanity publisher risks nothing. He gets his money up front *from you*, and he has no reputation in the business anyway.

However loud his protests to the contrary, he'll give you *no* editorial assessment, advice or service. He'll print your work exactly as you supply it, warts and all. He'll contract to bind only a small proportion of the copies you pay for, with an arrangement to print more as orders come in.

What orders? However many copies he sends out, you won't get any reviews. Vanity publishers' names are well known in the book trade. No reputable reviewer or publication will promote their products. With the possible exception of your small local bookshop, no bookseller will stock them.

So where does that leave you? Heavily out of pocket, disillusioned and disappointed. Probably angry. And left to do the selling yourself. There's always a risk, too, that you might not even have a book to sell.

One author's bitter experience
Writer Charles R Wickins, who lives in the Channel Islands, sent a short novel to a publisher called New Horizon, whose advertisements he had read. He didn't try to place the book anywhere else. The publisher accepted it at once. Mr Wickins's contract promised him 400 copies for about £1,600, to be paid in three instalments. Delighted to be given the chance to 'back his own horse', he sent the first instalment. Then the second. And he waited . . . and waited . . .

He was still waiting many months later when an anonymous 'friend' sent him a cutting from *Private Eye* which told him he'd been duped. Shortly after the *Private Eye* exposé, New Horizon's directors 'went abroad'. Mr Wickins never saw a single copy of his book, and never recovered a penny.

Be cautious about poetry, too
Alan Bond was an active campaigner for high standards in poetry. A well established writer and poet and a popular performer at festivals, Alan became increasingly perturbed in the last years of his life about the activities of some publishers who advertise for poetry to publish.

Putting one to the test, he wrote two poems in 28 seconds, before a witness, and sent them off under a pseudonym. Back came an offer to publish both poems – 'Just the kind of contemporary poems we're looking for' – in an anthology, if Alan would pay the publisher £7.50 for each poem published. In return, he would get copies of the anthology, one for each £7.50 paid. He would also have the privilege of buying more copies at 'only' £4.50 each.

Here are the spoof poems:

Flying Eyes

And then the bird
The big black
Bird
Flew towards my eyes.
I waved my arms
The bird flapped a wing
I let it go.

By Telecom

He rang.
I won't be long.
I waited.
He rang again.
The buses, the taxis, the
Excuses.
The door waits open.
I wait and wait and wait.

You can draw your own conclusions about the standard of selection applied by that 'publisher'. Would you be proud to see *your* work published alongside rubbish like that?

Don't risk your reputation

If you want to build up a reputation as a poet, steer well clear of paying to get your work published in an anthology. Avoid, too, those anthology competitions that have spread like a rash in recent years. No matter how good *your* poems might be, you'll have no control over the selection of the other poems. Your reputation could be badly tarnished, perhaps irretrievably.

Don't fall for these seductive advertisements. The risks are far too great.

YOUR SELF-PUBLISHING OPTIONS

Inexpensive methods

1. You could do the whole thing yourself, with a **typewriter** and access to a photocopier.

2. You could produce it on a **word processor** or **computer**.

3. Your could have your text typeset and printed by your **local 'instant print' shop**, and collate the pages yourself.

4. There might be a **community press** in your area, with printing equipment. Enquire at your library.

Read Jenny Vaughan's book *Getting into Print*, a practical guide covering techniques, design, production, sales and distribution.

If you have a little money to spend

For a fairly small outlay you could have your poems printed and made up into booklets or greeting cards. Your local printer will give you prices.

Joan B Howes has had many poems published in magazines, and also publishes her own poetry in booklets which she sells as fund-raisers, mainly for animal rescue. Her booklet *Orange and Sauce* has ten poems attractively printed on card. It cost Joan £75 for 100 copies, which she sold at a small profit through local bookshops. A review in her local paper helped to sell it. Besides raising a little money for a good cause, Joan finds the booklets make very acceptable small gifts, and provide a 'shop window' for her poetry.

Poems written in calligraphic handwriting on parchment or heavy paper then mounted in photoframes make popular gifts and sell well at craft fairs.

With a bit of imagination, you could have tea-towels or T-shirts produced. You'll find local companies who provide these services listed in *Yellow Pages*.

PUBLISHING YOUR OWN BOOK

There are several good books available to guide you through an ambitious venture like this. Going it alone can be well worth the effort. Harry Mulholland has certainly found this, with his successful series of mountain guidebooks:

> Self-publishing opens up exciting prospects of promoting projects in which you believe, with complete control of their design and content. Also production time is counted in months, not a year or more. To the usual ten per cent royalty you add the publisher's profit, and the postman can become your friend bringing orders or cheques – not rejected manuscripts.
>
> Harry Mulholland

Harry has put his own know-how and experience into his popular book *Guide to Self-Publishing – The A–Z of Getting Yourself into Print*. The book is self-published (of course), and you can get it through bookshops or direct from Harry's own publishing company Mulholland-Wirral at £7.95 including post and packing.

Recommendations

- Guide to *Self-Publishing – The A–Z of Getting Yourself into Print*, by Harry Mulholland – see above.

• *How to Publish Yourself* and *How to Publish Your Poetry* by Peter Finch. Practical guidance on every aspect of self-publishing from deciding to take the plunge to marketing your product.

• *Copy-editing* by Judith Butcher. The most comprehensive guide to professional copy preparation, the copy-editor's 'bible'.

• *Editing for Print* by Geoffrey Rogers. A guide to the business and technicalities of publishing, including the various editorial functions, book and magazine production methods, scheduling, budgeting, printing processes and a good deal more.

• *The Craft of Copywriting* and *Do Your Own Advertising*, both by Alastair Crompton. The skills and techniques of promoting and selling just about everything – and an eye-opening read about the advertising industry. These books have a special interest for the aspiring self-publisher. Both were originally published by the author as handsome hardbacks, and were so successful that Century Hutchinson bought the paperback rights.

• *How to Publish a Book* by Robert Spicer. The complete process of publishing a book, written by a successful independent publisher. A practical step-by-step guide to organising your project.

• *Bring It To Book* by Ann Kritzinger. A new book from an award-winning pioneer in short-run digital printing, written from 30 years' experience in publishing and print production.

A book production service
Book-in-Hand Ltd, run by Ann Kritzinger, is a print production service for self-publishers. The service includes design and editing advice, so customers have a better chance of selling in the open market.

Associations
There's an **Association of Little Presses**, which you can join to benefit from its members' advice and experience – see under Associations Open to Unpublished Writers at the back of this book.

Required by law

You are legally required to send one copy of your publication to **The Legal Deposit Office**, The British Library, Boston Spa, West Yorkshire LS28 7BY. A copy of every publication produced in the UK must be lodged there.

You'll eventually receive a demand from the **Agent for the Libraries** for a further five copies for distribution to the **copyright libraries** (Oxford, Cambridge, Dublin, Scotland and Wales). You won't get any payment for these six copies, but don't begrudge them too much. Their deposit with the libraries ensures that there is an official record of their existence, which might be useful in the event of any copyright problem. Also, it's to these libraries' lists that libraries throughout the English-speaking world look for potential additions to their own lists.

4
Writing Competitions

Cash prizes, publication, prestige, possibly fame – they're all on offer in the hundreds of writing competitions organised every year. Enter as many as you can (but have nothing to do with the anthology competitions mentioned in the previous chapter).

You never know what you can do...

Paul Heapy read about a science fiction short story competition being run by *The Sunday Times* jointly with publisher Victor Gollancz, who have a strong science fiction list. Intrigued by what he read, Paul decided to enter.

> They did the work for me. Had it been simply an SF story competition, no doubt I would not have entered. After all, I thought of myself as a poet. But J G Ballard wrote a superb introductory piece setting out his conception of what SF should be for. And great soul that he is, I could only agree. So when I won, it was just as though they had reached out and tapped me on the shoulder.
>
> Paul Heapy

Paul won first prize, his story was published, and Gollancz invited him to write a science fiction novel. He had never written *any kind* of short story before.

WHAT COULD YOU WIN?

Publication is the most sought-after prize of all. Competitions that guarantee publication of the winning entries attract by far the biggest postbags.

Most prizes are quite modest: a book token or a trophy, or a cash prize that might keep you in postage stamps – most cash prizes are between £25 and a few hundred pounds.

But you *might* win a spectacular sum like the prizes offered in the Arvon Foundation Biennial Poetry Competition, which amount to many thousands of pounds. There are also large prizes on offer for *unpublished* novels, for instance the Betty Trask Awards for a romantic first novel by a writer under 35, and the McKitterick Prize for an unpublished or a first published novel by an author over 40 years of age.

Have a go at the big ones

Don't be put off entering big competitions by the thought of all the famous writers you might be up against. Entries are often judged on a 'no name on the entry' basis, especially big poetry competitions. The judges don't know who wrote what till the adjudication is complete. There are several ways of organising this, and each competition carries details of its required method in its literature and entry forms.

In practice, however, a very big competition is more a lottery than a contest. The usual procedure is that the entries are divided up among a panel of adjudicators. Each chooses what he considers to be the best entries from his batch, then all the judges read all the short-listed manuscripts *only*. So if a judge eliminates your entry in the first round, no one else will see it.

From the short-list, each judge selects his potential winners, and the eventual winners are chosen from these survivors – sometimes with a good deal of heat. Philip Larkin once said in public that the poem his fellow judges of a major poetry competition had selected as the overall winner didn't make good sense.

WHAT DO THE JUDGES LOOK FOR?

In **short-story competitions**, the same qualities a fiction editor looks for:

- a story that grabs and holds the reader's interest
- a story that stimulates the desire to know 'what happens next'
- a story that is soundly structured
- a story that is fluently written.

Note, a *story*. One of the most common faults, judges say, is that many writers don't really understand what a short story is and what it is not – see Chapter 8.

In **poetry competitions**, the qualities an adjudicator looks for were summarised by the late Howard Sergeant MBE, who was founding-editor of *Outposts Poetry Quarterly* for over 40 years. Howard's criteria are reproduced here by kind permission of his widow, Jean. They are:

- craftsmanship
- adequate command of the tone and language appropriate to the poem in question
- individual vision and use of imagination
- genuine feeling and personal contact.

In **plays**, the criteria used by the judges vary enormously because of the differences in the facilities and economics of the companies that organise them. Each competition should indicate its requirements in its literature, and it will be an advantage to make yourself familiar with the venue where the winning plays might eventually be performed, to avoid obviously impossible special effects and staging.

ENTERING WRITING COMPETITIONS

The DOs
1. *Do* read the rules. That's obvious, you say? You would be surprised to see how many people don't bother. Yet it's foolish to risk instant elimination in this way. If you infringe *any* of the rules, you're out – and no one will send back your entry fee.

2. *Do* respect the set word or line limits. If you don't, the judges *will* notice because they are bound by the rules, too. They won't risk the wrath of other competitors by awarding the prize to a piece that's either too long or too short according to the rules.

3. *Do* write what is asked for. Some writers don't seem to realise that, for instance, an article entered for a short-story competition will be thrown out at once. They're wasting their time and their entry fees.

4. *Do* study your 'market'. If the prize includes publication, it makes sense to study the magazine or newspaper that will print the winners, to make sure your entry is appropriate. Publication in a national women's or 'family' magazine would rule out explicit sex, violence, or over-strong language.

5. *Do* keep a copy of your entry, whether or not the original will be returned (and most competitions don't return entries).

6. *Do* stick to the standard ms layouts, unless the rules say otherwise.

7. *Do* remember that judges, like editors, are human (yes, truly), and could be put off by a badly presented entry.

And the DON'Ts

1. *Don't* be tempted to enter any competition that requires you to give up your copyright. However attractive the prizes, you could be signing away your rights to long-term benefits. Your poem might become a favourite for anthologies or even school text-books, your short story might be adapted for radio or TV – it might even become the basis for a series – and you would have no claim at all to *any* payment.

2. *Don't* wrap your entry up in elaborate packaging. Fancy folders, decorated cover-sheets, ribbon bows and suchlike are just a nuisance to the organisers, and will go straight into the waste bucket. One organiser remarked that she had received a Jiffy-bag containing a cardboard document wallet inside which was a mass of tissue paper covering a plastic sleeve, all to protect a single poem. It's odd, too, how the fanciest packaging, according to adjudicators' reports, almost invariably contains the worst entries.

3. *Don't* forget to enclose your entry fee. Your entry will be disqualified without it, and the organisers are unlikely to go to the trouble and expense of sending you a reminder.

4. *Don't* be too devastated if you don't win. Remember that all competitions are a lottery to some extent. Just keep trying. It's wonderful practice in writing to set lengths about set subjects – and remember Paul Heapy.

CHECKLIST

Check these points before you send off a competition entry:

1. Have you read *all* the rules?

2. Is your entry appropriate to the competition subject?
3. Is your entry suitable for publication (if applicable)?
4. Does it comply with the stipulated lengths?
5. Have you typed it in the standard layout on white A4 paper?
6. Have you kept a copy?
7. Have you understood and followed any special instructions about anonymous entry and so on?
8. Have you enclosed the correct entry fee, and made your cheque or postal order payable to the designated name?
9. Have you enclosed an SAE if one was requested?

FINDING OUT MORE

• Writers' circles, literary groups and creative writing classes receive regular information.

• Your local library probably has leaflets. If none are on display, ask at the information desk – some organisers ask for their leaflets to be kept for those interested enough to enquire, rather than left out to be picked up and used as shopping-list scrap-paper by browsers.

• Writers' magazines like *Writers' Bulletin, Writers News, Writers' Forum* and *The New Writer* list current and forthcoming competitions.

• The *Friends of Arvon* newsletter has a competitions column.

• The *Writers' & Artists' Yearbook* and *The Writer's Handbook* list major literary awards.

• The Book Trust Information Service.

• The Poetry Library.

• Flyers distributed by literary and poetry magazines.

• National newspapers and magazines carry notices of major competitions, and some run their own.

5
Writing for Magazines and Newspapers

WRITING ARTICLES

Take a look at your newsagent's shelves. Did you realise that nearly all the publications you see there buy most of their articles from freelance writers?

The constant demand for good articles makes them one of the easiest types of writing to sell. Easier to sell, however, doesn't mean easier to write. The demand is high, certainly, but the standard expected is also high.

Potential outlets

There are literally thousands of potential outlets for articles. The *Writers' & Artists' Yearbook* lists over 600 UK newspapers and magazines that publish (and pay for) articles. *Willing's Press Guide* lists more than 10,000 UK publications, including trade, professional and specialist magazines, and many of these welcome freelance contributions relevant to their subject areas.

Writers' Bulletin carries in-depth information about editors' current 'wants'. The Bureau of Freelance Photographers' *Market Newsletter* carries market information geared specifically to photojournalism.

To write and sell freelance articles, you need:

- the ability to write clear, concise English
- an observant eye
- an enquiring mind
- a professional approach to writing up your material.

To succeed at article writing, you must study a market regularly – editors' needs change – and slant your writing to meet that requirement.

Start off with a good strong 'hook' and try to end strongly too.

For a saleable writing style, keep words, sentences and paragraphs short and simple. And keep on writing.

Gordon Wells

A MANY-SPLENDOURED MEDIUM

Never mind how new you are to writing, there's sure to be at least one facet of article-writing that could give you your first taste of publication. Look at the choice:

- factual articles
- personal experiences
- human interest stories
- opinion pieces
- 'how-to' and DIY articles
- 'round-up' articles (where a number of people contribute ideas/ experiences/opinions)
- self-help and self-improvement
- interviews
- profiles
- short-short articles and fillers
- and you'll probably add more as you explore the possibilities.

Make it shapely

Whatever your subject, an article needs to be structured into a logical and satisfying form. Like a good story, it needs a beginning, a middle and an end. But unlike a story, where you can take liberties with that order of things, an article works best with the most straightforward sequence:

1. **A strong opening paragraph**. If you've dug up some amazing or little-known fact, or if you have a strong statement to make, put it here. For example, you might open an article on *Writing as a Second Career* with: 'Politician Edwina Currie spends her spare time writing sexy and scandalous political novels – and she gets them published. How many other famous people have a writing career as a second string?'

   It's a common misjudgement for beginners to save their juiciest fact till the end. But if you don't grab your reader's interest right away he might not bother to read to the end, so your astonishing revelation is lost. Feed your reader the tastiest titbit first, and save the second-best to the last.

2. **The middle**, the main course. This should be packed with interesting information written in the most logical sequence, but not presented simply as a list of facts. Spice it with anecdotes, questions, opinions.

3. **The closing paragraph.** This should provide a satisfying round-off, summarising in some way what you've been saying. It's a good idea to refer back, however obliquely, to your first paragraph: 'Given the chance, would Mrs Currie give up politics to write full-time?'

If you do have another interesting fact to offer, you could conclude with that: 'Agatha Christie's main career was writing. So was her second string. She wrote six romantic-psychological novels under the pen-name of Mary Westmacott. She wrote in her *Autobiography* that these novels were the only ones that really satisfied her. Her crime novels were her bread and butter.'

Shorts and short-shorts

The terms 'short articles' and 'short-short articles' sometimes puzzle new writers. These terms don't really have any strict definitions. What would be considered a short article by one magazine might be a full-length feature to another. Generally speaking, though, you can work on the basis that:

- A **short-short article** is under 500 words.
- A **short article** is 500–700 words.
- An **article** is usually 750–2,000 words.

Always check the length preferences of any particular market as a matter of course, before you send them any material.

Fillers

A **filler** is a short item fitted into a small space so that a page won't be left with blank paper where the main items don't quite fill it.

Anecdotes, humorous verse, puzzles, jokes, cartoons, tips and hints, press errors, odd facts, brain-teasers, quotations – all these are used as fillers, and many magazines buy them from freelances.

Keep an eye open for likely filler slots, and collect odd pieces of information, jokes, 'overheards' and suchlike.

Readers' letters

These, too, come into the category of fillers, but they've acquired a status of their own and are now a strong selling feature for many magazines and newspapers.

Payment can be as high as £50, but the average is £5 to £10 (higher where photographs are used) and some magazines 'pay' in prizes instead of cash.

The 'Letters to the Editor' slot is a popular starting point for many new writers. Don't be misled into thinking that because they're short they're easy to write and sell. A successful letter has probably been worked on just as carefully as any article – it has to be tailored to its market, too.

Every publication has its own style. Look at points like:

• Does the publication prefer long or short letters?

• Is the tone of the letters neutral? cosy? argumentative? cynical? amused? helpful? sympathetic? belligerent?

• Do any of the letters raise controversial issues?

• Are any of the letters obvious responses to correspondence or features that appeared in previous issues of the publication?

Readers' letters are good practice for an aspiring article-writer because they demand the same kind of disciplines: no waffle, no wordiness, and they must make their point as clearly and concisely as possible.

You can use pen-names if you like. Editors might not want to see the same names appearing too often in their letters pages.

SAE not usually required
'Readers' letters' is one area where the convention of enclosing an SAE doesn't usually apply. Letters are seldom returned, and most are only acknowledged if they're used. No voucher copies are sent. You *might* get advance notice, or you might hear nothing at all till you receive your payment.

A book to help you
Alison Chisholm's book *How to Write Five-Minute Features* shows you how to write successful 'Letters to the Editor', plus puzzles, ultra-short fiction and filler material.

WRITER'S BLOCK

Before we go on to look at the various types of writing, let's take the mystique out of this much-discussed 'affliction'.

Sometimes called 'frozen brain syndrome', writer's block is all too often a self-inflicted problem. You stare at the blank page. You *want* to write. You drink a third cup of strong coffee. Still nothing comes. Why?

The reasons are seldom mysterious, muse-dependent or beyond your control. Ask yourself the following questions relevant to what you're trying to write:

Non-fiction

1. Do you **care** about your subject? Does it move you, excite, annoy, thrill, disturb, infuriate, inspire you? Do you really have something to say about it?

2. Or did you choose it because it looked like a potentially **marketable** topic? It didn't look too challenging? Because you were stuck for any other ideas? Because you feel it doesn't much matter *what* you write as long as you write *something*?

3. Assuming you do have something to say, have you **researched** the subject thoroughly, and formulated your own ideas about it?

Fiction

1. Do you really *want* to write fiction? Or do you equate 'being a writer' with 'being a fiction-writer'? (Be honest – you won't succeed if your heart isn't in it – and editors can usually tell.)

2. Assuming that fiction *is* your field, have you taken time to think about your **characters** – what kind of people they are, what has made them that way, what they want, how they're likely to behave, how they'll react to and interact with each other in the situations you plan for them?

3. Have you prepared a convincing **background**, from knowledge and experience and/or research?

4. Have you experimented till you've found the right **storytelling viewpoint** and character?

5. Have you allowed **time** for your story to simmer, to build in your mind till it's boiling over and you can't wait another minute to get it down on paper?

In other words, are you trying to write either something that's more of a chore than a pleasure, or something that is not yet ready to be written? In most cases, writer's block results from either lack of involvement or lack of preparation. The cure is in your own hands.

CHOOSING YOUR TOPIC

Your best bet if you're a beginner is to write about something you know well. The better you know your subject the more confidently you'll handle it, and your confidence will communicate itself to your reader. Remember that the first reader who will see your article is an editor. An experienced editor senses at once if a writer is trying to tackle a subject he isn't really comfortable with.

From your knowledge of the subject, you're probably already familiar with the publications that might be interested in publishing your articles. Armed with that familiarity, you should be able to write more than one article on your subject, slanting each to a different market.

For instance, if your hobby is collecting old gramophone records, you could write about:

• where to find them
• how to store them
• how much they cost
• the equipment needed to play them
• the artists who made them

.... and much, much more, as the subject diagram in Figure 8 shows.

Try making your own subject diagram. Write down the main subject in the middle of a (large) sheet of paper, and write its main branches all round it. You'll quickly see how the branches begin to shoot out sub-branches, and probably even the sub-branches could produce twigs. This kind of lateral thinking (sometimes called 'mind-mapping') is far more productive than simply making a linear list. It's a powerful brainstormer.

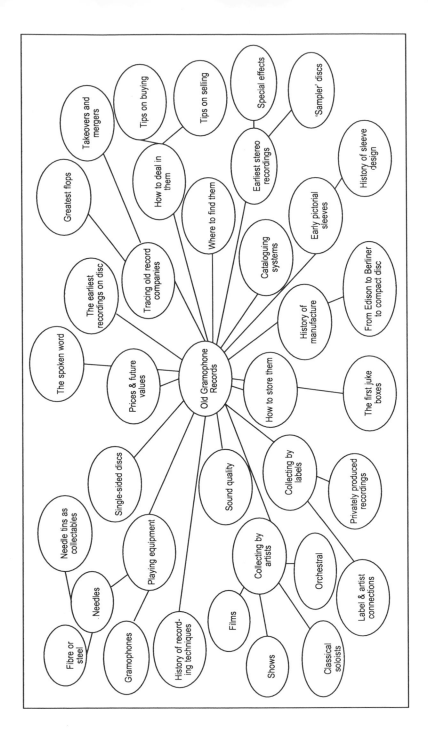

Fig. 8. Making a subject diagram.

What do you know already?

You can use the same exercise to map out sources of information on your subject, and on possible markets. You'll find ideas coming almost faster than you can write them down.

Make it convincing

Whatever your subject, make it your business to gather enough information and solid facts about it to write a convincing, fact-packed article. The editorial nose will quickly sniff out a 'scissors-and-paste' job – that is, a piece cobbled together from reference books and other people's opinions. Of course, you can make use of other people's findings and conclusions (provided you don't infringe their copyright), but your article will be stillborn if it contains little or nothing of your own thoughts and feelings about the subject.

You'll often find, too, that it will take several rewrites to achieve a convincingly 'spontaneous' style. And don't be afraid to let your own personality show through.

Be methodical

You'll save yourself a lot of irritation, time and trouble, if you devise a simple system for filing your article and filler information as you gather it. It's infuriating if you're stuck for one small piece of information and you can't remember where you put it.

You need to be able to retrieve information quickly and easily the minute you want it. This is especially important if you're trying to fit your writing into precious spare time sandwiched between your day job and keeping the weeds down.

You can use document wallets, large envelopes, card index systems or, of course, electronic storage if you have a computer (don't forget to back everything up). The system itself doesn't matter – what *does* matter is that you have one.

Don't let research take over your writing time, though. As Gordon Wells says in *The Craft of Writing Articles*: 'You need to be able to find facts quickly and easily. But your hobby is writing – make sure it does not become "fact-filing".'

Where to look for information

- Your local library. If you tell the library staff what you're looking for and why you want it, you'll find them very helpful.

- *Research for Writers* by Ann Hoffmann is an indispensable source of information about how and where to find information.

- Newspaper cuttings. There are lists of press cutting agencies in the *Writers' & Artists' Yearbook* and *The Writer's Handbook*. Such agencies are not cheap, but a subscription could be an excellent investment, especially if you specialise.

- Specialist book dealers. There might be one locally – look in *Yellow Pages* or ask at the library. Many advertise in the *Book and Magazine Collector*.

- **The British Library Newspaper Library** at Colindale, North London, houses London newspapers from 1901, and English provincial, Scottish, Irish, Commonwealth and foreign newspapers from 1700. You need to apply to the Library for a reader's pass.

SELLING YOUR ARTICLES

It's usual now to send a **query letter** before you submit an article. This has long been the accepted practice in the US, and most American editors insist on a preliminary query. Sending in material 'over the transom' is actively discouraged.

In general in the UK, though, you can still send in a very short article – up to about 500 words – as a complete ms. It would take an editor nearly as long to read a query letter as it does to scan a short piece. You won't get a firm acceptance on the strength of a query anyway, unless the editor knows your work already, so you might as well let him see what you can do. If he prefers a preliminary query, he'll let you know.

Longer pieces are another matter. You should query the editor first, and not solely to save time and postage. If the editor is interested he might have some suggestions to make about your treatment of the subject, perhaps asking you to take a different approach to the topic, or to make the piece shorter than you suggested, and so on.

Writing a query letter
Your query letter should tell the editor three things:

1. The **subject** of the article and the **angle** you intend to treat it from. Use the 'bullet' system to list your points briefly and clearly, and indicate the proposed length.

2. Why you think his readers would be interested in what you have to say.

3. Why *you* are able and qualified to write it. If you have special
    qualifications – practical experience, a degree in the subject, or
    something like that – include them here, but avoid dragging in
    qualifications, however impressive, that are totally irrelevant to
    the subject you'll be writing about. If you're offering an article
    on, say, collecting Commonwealth commemorative stamps,
    your target editor is unlikely to rush off an enthusiastic
    response because you've told him you've been practising yoga
    and transcendental meditation for 20 years.

Suppose you want to offer the editor of a general interest
magazine an article on collecting ephemera, those throw-away bits
of social history: postcards, programmes, tickets, bookmarks and
the like. First, check that you have the current editor's name,
correctly spelled. Then structure your query something like the letter
in Figure 9.

BOOKS TO HELP YOU

• Lisa Collier Cool, *How To Sell Every Magazine Article You Write.*
  An American book on the techniques of selling by query letter
  before you write the article. This approach has long been the
  norm in America and UK editors are rapidly adopting the
  requirement to query rather than sending the complete piece.

• Anthony Davis, *Magazine Journalism Today.* Follows magazine
  production from planning to publication, including much useful
  insight and advice on how material is commissioned and how it is
  best written, both by in-house staff and freelances. Enlightening
  analyses of what makes good features and interviews. Covers
  research as well as writing.

• Jill Dick, *Writing for Magazines.* A comprehensive guide covering
  the whole magazine field from mainstream to small presses and
  specialist markets, as well as research, rights, keeping records, tax
  matters, syndication and more.

• Connie Emerson, *The 30-minute Writer.* Practical advice on
  writing short pieces – one-page articles, opinion pieces, profiles,
  humour – in half-hour bites of time.

Emily Hoarder
White Elephants
Overflow Lane
Fillingham

10 October 199X

David Payer
Editor
Take-Anything magazine
Anytown S1 1XX

Dear Mr Payer

I am writing to enquire whether you would be interested in seeing
an article about collecting ephemera.

There is plenty of scope in this field for building up an interesting
and potentially valuable collection, without too great a financial
outlay. Many of your readers might not know how collectable these
scraps of social history have become. Some might not even know
that such a field of collecting exists.

To begin a collection they would need to know:

- what the term 'ephemera' means: essentially items of no
  intrinsic value, such as postcards, cigarette cards, bookmarks,
  tickets, magazines and newspapers, advertising material,
  pamphlets and so on
- where to look for collectable items: antique and collectors' fairs,
  where a few dealers specialise in ephemera, jumble sales,
  charity shops, the attics and cellars of friends and relations . . .
- approximate prices they might expect to pay
- where the best potential lies for increases in value
- the best ways to store and/or display their collection.

Once a new collector begins to realise how wide the range is, he
or she often moves on to specialisation, and is soon hooked on the
hobby. It's fun, it's fascinating, and it's relatively inexpensive.

I have been collecting ephemera myself for several years, and have
recently begun to specialise in bookmarks, their design and history,
and their value to the companies that issued them (they were
widely used as an advertising medium).

The text as I plan it would be 1,750–2,000 words, and I can supply
a variety of photographs, if you wish.

I enclosed a stamped addressed envelope for your reply.

Yours sincerely

(Mrs) Emily Hoarder

Fig. 9. Writing a query letter.

86

- Brendan Hennessy, *Writing Feature Articles*. A practical guide to writing successful features – how to gather, organise and target information.

- John Morrison, *Freelancing for Magazines: A Guide for Writers and Photographers*. Delivers exactly what it promises. Articulate, comprehensive and thorough.

- Gordon Wells, *The Magazine Writer's Handbook*. Lists specific magazine markets, giving editorial requirements and so on. Useful as a guide, but make sure you only use the latest edition. Even then, check the information, because the magazine scene is so volatile that some entries might be out of date almost before the ink is dry.

- Gordon Wells, *Photography for Article Writers*. A practical guide to taking the kind of photographs that will help you sell more articles. Like all Gordon's books, it's thoroughly sensible and down to earth, and an enjoyable read, too.

- Leonard Witt (editor) *The Complete Book of Feature Writing*. Covers Personality Profiles, Travel Articles, How Tos, Criticism and Reviews, Human Interest . . . Guaranteed to get your fingers itching for the keyboard.

LOOKING AT JOURNALISM

A successful journalist is a writer who knows how to:

- tell his story within tightly focused limits
- see his story from his reader's angle
- avoid verbosity and cut out padding
- express his meaning in clear, concise and unambiguous language
- produce quality work under pressure, to meet tight deadlines.

Robbie Gray is a former chief sub-editor/night-editor of the *Daily Mirror*, *Daily Express*, *Sunday People* and *The Star*. Asked what advice he would offer to aspiring journalists, Robbie said:

I have only to repeat the advice of Sir Hugh Cudlipp when he was editor of the *Daily Mirror*: 'Keep it simple.'

It was also Cudlipp who said: 'Never talk down to your reader.' It took me some time in my salad days to work out precisely what he meant – and, of course, it was exactly that. Never try to give the readers the impression that you think you are cleverer than they are. Never deliberately try to send them scurrying off in search of a dictionary. They don't have time, and probably won't bother.

Robbie Gray

Most newspapers, like most magazines, buy material from freelance writers. There are three main types of newspaper: national, regional and local. The *Writers' & Artists' Yearbook* lists all the nationals and a few of the regionals, but *The Writer's Handbook* gives more information in this field, listing all the major national and regional titles, with editorial names and requirements, tips about approaching them, and what they pay.

The financial rewards

Payment varies a good deal. Some papers pay NUJ (National Union of Journalists) rates whether you're a union member or not. Others pay 'by arrangement', in which case you'll be offered what the editor thinks the piece is worth, or possibly, if he's never heard of you, what he thinks you'll be prepared to settle for. This is one of the areas where a thoroughly professional approach can really pay off. Don't invite the editor to offer you less than he might have done because your badly presented and carelessly spelled ms and your tatty recycled envelopes leave him in no doubt that he's dealing with someone who doesn't know the business.

Unless you're already a member of the NUJ, there's little use in arguing about the offer. You can either refuse it and try your luck elsewhere, or you can accept it philosophically so that you can add another item to your portfolio of published work. A strong portfolio will eventually put you in a position to negotiate fees, as more and more publications are asking for clips of previously published work to be included with proposals.

NUJ rates go up to about £210 + per 1,000 words for a feature in a national daily newspaper, and about £315 + per 1,000 words in a national Sunday newspaper. You could add 50 per cent to these figures for exclusive coverage of a topical item. Provincial papers pay much less, but they should pay *something* – you won't be doing yourself or other writers any favours if you write for nothing.

Getting your foot in the door

Local papers are your best bet to begin with. They always want:

- news stories, short and to the point, covering local events: 'Her majesty unveils memorial plaque', 'local grandmother's surprise triplets'

- social issue articles: 'Save our swimming baths!', 'Do our citizens want clean streets?'

- striking photographs of local people, places and events. (Notice the strong 'local' emphasis.)

The five 'W's

When you're writing your article, make sure you don't omit any essential information. Check the content against the journalist's creed, the five 'W's:

- Who?

- What?

- Where?

- When?

- Why?

And if it's appropriate, add an 'H' – How?

Whether distributed free or not, these papers live on their advertising revenue, so short pieces stand a better chance of acceptance because they leave more room for ads.

Include a photograph or two with your article if you can. Check with the paper about preferred sizes and films.

Find out, too, about deadlines – this week's hot news is next week's rejection.

You'll usually be paid after publication, at some set date, and you might be expected to submit an **invoice**. Clarify this beforehand. An invoice is a simple business document, a bill asking for payment of money which is due to you. It's easy to prepare. Just make sure you include all the necessary information, as in Figure 10.

```
                        Invoice
                                        Oliver Columnist
                                        12 Gossip Alley
                                        Tiny Tiles
                                        By Eastborough
22 July 199X

Basil Bond
Editor
Eastborough Tattle
Eastborough

To writing one short feature, 'Scandal at the
Vicarage', published in Eastborough Tattle
15.7.9X                                 £25.00
```

Fig. 10. Example of an invoice.

Articles have to be straightforward and to the point – there is little room for picturesque speech. Most important of all, facts should be absolutely accurate. Dates should be given where applicable, since while it may be obvious to you that last Sunday means last Sunday, in the chaos of an editor's office such things cannot be taken for granted. Dated material gets first priority, and in any case it is professional procedure. If I ever quote anyone then I usually enclose a separate sheet giving details of how they can be contacted, and then the editor can verify or expand an interview, or perhaps arrange a photograph.

Give names and dates in full. There should be no reason for the editor to think you haven't done your job properly.

Writing factual pieces imposes its own discipline on the writer, and this is particularly healthy for those writers who are just starting off.

Graham Thomas

You're never too young to start writing for publication. Graham Thomas started at 15, and was soon selling regularly to his local papers. He studied English and Philosophy at university, and hopes to make writing his full-time career.

Is there a gap in the coverage?

If you spot an opening for a topic your paper isn't already covering, you could suggest ideas, perhaps for:

- a book, film, TV or video column
- a poetry corner
- a children's page
- an original series that *you* could supply on a regular basis.

But don't suggest any kind of competition unless you're willing to handle the entries yourself. The staff won't welcome the extra work.

More books

Freelance Writing for Newspapers is a very helpful handbook written by Jill Dick, who has been a journalist all her working life. From her experience both as a staff journalist (on *The Sun*, the *News of the World* and the *Manchester Evening News*) and as a highly successful freelancer, Jill gives the kind of practical advice and information that is invaluable to every writer who wants to write for the press.

Jill Dick's book *Writing for Magazines* is a useful and popular complement to *Freelance Writing for Newspapers*.

Joan Clayton's *Journalism for Beginners* has much to offer the experienced writer as well as the beginner. It's brimful of advice and ideas to get you going.

6
Writing a Non-Fiction Book

Are you an expert on a subject that would interest a large number of people? Do you have first-hand experience or knowledge that might benefit, profit, intrigue, amuse or inspire others? Have you set up and run a successful business? Built your own house? Prospected for gold in the Andes? Perhaps then you've already thought of writing a book about it, but didn't know where to begin.

IS YOUR IDEA FEASIBLE?

Before you commit yourself to the project and all the hard work it will involve, ask yourself these questions:

1. Is the subject big enough for a book? *An Encyclopedia of Houseplant Care* would be. *How to Water Your Aspidistra* wouldn't.

2. Would the subject interest a wide enough readership to make it a commercial proposition? Books do get written and published on some pretty obscure topics, but they're usually intended for a specialist market. It depends on how wide a readership you want to reach, and on whether it's mainly profit or prestige you want. It also depends on finding the right publisher for your subject. There are many publishers who might want an *A–Z of Microwave Cookery*, but not many who would take on, for instance, *Advanced Theory of Semi-Conductors*.

3. Is the subject one that will attract the book-buying public as well as library stockists? The biggest potential sales are in books on self-improvement (both physical and psychological), health, food and diet, leisure activities and hobbies. Do-it-yourself titles sell well, and books on cookery and gardening waltz off the shelves. 'How-to' books are in constant demand, especially those that show how to make or save money. An American

publisher, asked by a beginning writer if he thought anyone would ever write *the* 'Great American Novel', advised: 'Forget the Great American Novel. What this country needs is a good book on how to repair your own car.'

You've got a suitable subject – so how do you tackle it?

First, break it down into manageable sections. The prospect of getting 30,000 words or more down on paper can be pretty daunting. Split it up into ten or twelve chapters of about 3,000 words each, and it loses much of its terror. It becomes more like writing a series of articles on your topic.

Divide your subject on paper, then, into ten or twelve sub-themes. These will eventually form your chapters. Under each sub-theme heading note all the information you already have that's relevant to that section. Make notes of any obvious gaps in that information (different coloured inks will help). You'll have to do some research to fill those gaps.

Now comes the crunch
Do you have, or do you know how and where to find, enough material to write each of your chapters – at least 2,500 words – *without waffle or padding*? Can you realistically expect to pack every chapter with interesting and relevant information?

If not, abandon it, and look for a more substantial subject. Don't throw away your notes, though. You've probably got enough material there for several articles at least.

If you're sure there's enough solid material, enough factual information for a book, then go ahead and prepare your proposal.

But don't write the book yet. If you don't find a taker for your idea, you don't want to have wasted your time writing an unsaleable book. And if a publisher does express an interest, he might want to make suggestions about the way you write the book – perhaps a different kind of treatment from the one you originally envisaged, or a format to fit an existing list. If you'd already written the whole book, you would then have to do an extensive rewrite.

PREPARING A PROPOSAL

First, make an **outline** of the complete book. Set down your title. The publisher might want to change it, but for the purposes of the proposal you need a **working title**. Make it as snappy as you can. *Raising Funds for Charity* is more effective than *Organising*

Part of an outline for a proposed book – *Raising Funds for Charity*

Introduction
A short general overview of the choices for raising funds as an individual, a small group, or a larger group run by a committee. It will also draw attention to the need to know how the law affects various activities – this will be covered in one of the chapters.

Chapter 1: How to set up a committee
This will show the various offices – chairperson, secretary, treasurer and so on – and will define each office and the responsibilities it usually carries, stressing the importance of allocating the right job to the right person. For instance, it's hopeless to appoint as Treasurer someone who can't tell an invoice from a receipt.

Chapter 2: Fund raising and the law
What you need to know about what you can do without permission, what you need permission for – for instance, you can't sell raffle tickets door-to-door without a special permit – and what you can't do at all.

Chapter 3: Drawing up a provisional programme of events
Your committee needs to decide what is within its members' capabilities and what isn't. For instance, there's no point in trying to organise a jumble sale if your members are not willing to sort out the jumble. It's no good, either, deciding to have a brass band concert if the nearest brass band is based a hundred miles away and you would have to meet its travelling expenses.

This chapter will include a list of suggestions for events: a summer fair, a Christmas craft fair, an antiques and collectables fair, a car boot sale, a raffle, an auction, a dinner dance and dozens more.

It will also point out the areas where you need special insurance and safety precautions.

Fig. 11. Outline for a proposed book.

Synopsis: *Raising Funds for Charity*

The book will cover all aspects of fund-raising, from individual efforts (making and selling crafts, holding a coffee morning, hosting a sales party and so on) to large committee-run, business-sponsored events like dinner dances and concerts.

It will be spiced with accounts of real-life achievements – I know of a man who raised many thousands of pounds for a hospital by hiring Concorde and flying a party to the USA – which will intrigue, encourage and inspire the reader.

Legal, health and safety aspects will all be covered. There will be suggestions for a comprehensive range of money-making possibilities, and a directory of contact addresses: services, suppliers, information sources and so on.

I believe that there are many people who would be attracted by having so much information offered in one handy volume. It would be helpful both to individuals and to organisations: clubs and societies, schools and colleges, hospital support groups, church groups and many more.

As far as I have been able to ascertain, there are very few publications on the open market that gather together so many facts and suggestions and combine them with an interesting and entertaining narrative.

And one of the essential ingredients for success in any enterprise is surely that the participants should enjoy the venture from the outset. The necessary literature should also be part of the enjoyment.

Fig. 12. Typical synopsis for a proposed book.

Successful Events to Raise Money for Charitable Projects. It would fit the spine of the book better, too.

Write down the first chapter heading, and set out underneath it, briefly, all the points you intend to deal with in that chapter. List all your chapters in this way. (Index cards are useful here.) Then juggle the chapters into a logical sequence. This is the skeleton of your book, the bones on which you'll build the meat.

Type the outline neatly in single spacing, like a letter (this is a document, not a working typescript). An extract from such a document is shown in Figure 11. Indicate the proposed overall length of the book (the 'extent'). If illustrations are appropriate, say whether or not you can supply them. The publisher will advise you if he prefers to make arrangements for illustrations himself.

The synopsis and sales pitch

On a separate sheet of paper, type out:

• a short, concise explanation of the book's proposed purpose and area of interest

• why you believe there's a need for it

• what market you envisage for it

• a few words to show you know what the competition is like

• why you believe *your* book will be better.

Be sure to keep copies of these papers. An example of a synopsis is given in Figure 12.

APPROACHING A PUBLISHER

Look through the publishers listed in the *Writers' & Artists' Yearbook* and *The Writer's Handbook* and draw up a list of those who specify an interest in books of the kind you plan.

Before you go any further, ask at your library if they can access a **writers' database** on computer or if they have a copy of Whitaker's *British Books in Print*. You need to find out which of your target companies have recently published a book on your subject. Unless you can offer something radically different in your handling of the subject, you would be at a disadvantage with these publishers. Book Trust Information Service can help here, too.

Decide which publisher you'll approach first. If you possibly can, find out the name of the editor responsible for the type of non-fiction book you want to offer. Ring the company's switchboard and ask the operator. If the operator doesn't know, ask to be put through to the editorial department for non-fiction books. Ask whoever you speak to there for the appropriate name, and make sure you know how to spell it. Don't try to discuss the book on the phone unless you are specifically asked to do so – all you want at this stage is the right name, so you can be sure your proposal will reach the right person as quickly as possible. *The Writer's Handbook* includes many editors' names as contacts in the various houses listed there, but it's as well to check up, as publishing personnel move about a lot.

Your covering letter

This should be brief and to the point. All the information about your proposed book is in your proposal, so there's no need to repeat any of it in the letter.

If you have any special qualifications for writing the book, you should mention these – but only mention *relevant* matters. Your degree in metaphysics won't persuade an editor to accept your book about fund-raising – it has no relevance. Your experience in the field does, though. All you need is something on the lines of:

Dear Mr Corn-Harvester
I enclose a synopsis and outline of a book I am preparing about fund-raising for charity. I've had 15 years of experience in this field, both in active organisation and in administration. Would you be interested in seeing the manuscript?
Yours sincerely

Send the letter with the outline and synopsis, and remember to enclose an SAE.

Prepare a sample chapter or two

You might have to wait a while for a reply, or you might have to try several publishers before you get a nibble of interest. Spend this waiting time working on a couple of sample chapters and on gathering information you're going to need to fill the gaps you identified when you were making your original notes.

When a publisher does express interest, he'll probably ask you to send him at least one chapter, to see whether or not the content will live up to the promise of the proposal. He'll also want to assess your capabilities as a writer before he commits himself, so you must make your sample as good as you possibly can.

When you're offered an agreement

If your sample is satisfactory, the publisher will either ask to see the completed ms 'on spec' (in which case you should think very carefully before committing yourself to finishing the book with no definite prospect of acceptance) or he will offer you an agreement on the strength of what he has already seen. With the agreement, he *might* also offer you an advance against royalties.

The *offer* of a book contract entitles you to apply for membership of The Society of Authors and/or The Writers' Guild of Great Britain. Either of these organisations will advise you about the agreement you've been offered, so as soon as you receive the document, contact them and they'll scrutinise it on your behalf, *before you sign it*.

You should read up on contracts. The Society of Authors' *Quick Guide to Publishing Contracts* is very helpful; Michael Legat's *An Author's Guide to Publishing* and Barry Turner's *The Writer's Companion* will also help you understand contracts.

BOOKS TO HELP YOU

- Anthony Blond, *The Book Book*. Gives an insider's view of the publishing world, and shows how saleable mss are selected.

- Giles N Clark, *Inside Book Publishing*. Aimed at those seeking a career in publishing. Shows what publishing house staff actually do in the production of books from blockbusters to academic texts, including the finding and developing of publishable books.

- Michael Legat, *An Author's Guide to Publishing* and *Writing for Pleasure and Profit*. Both good on this topic, and also on contracts.

- Gordon Wells, *How to Write Non-Fiction Books*, *The Book Writer's Handbook*, *The Successful Author's Handbook* and *Writers' Questions Answered*. Practical down-to-earth advice, and common-sense strategies for getting non-fiction published.

- Norman Toulson, *Writing a Nonfiction Book*. How to seize and hold your readers' attention 'as firmly as the author of a whodunnit'.

- Penny Grubb and Danuta Reah, *Writing a Textbook*. How to write 'tools of the trade' for educators, trainers, researchers and students.

SOME PUBLISHERS WITH STRONG NON-FICTION LISTS

● **Aurum Press Ltd**: high quality illustrated and non-illustrated adult non-fiction in general human interest, art and craft, lifestyle and travel.

● **Cassell**: business and general non-fiction.

● **B T Batsford Ltd**: chess, lacecraft, hobbies, animal care, fashion and costume, photography, sport, games, theatre, transport, travel.

● **Kyle Cathie Ltd**: history, natural history, health, biography, food and drink, craft, gardening, reference.

● **The Crowood Press Ltd**: animal and land husbandry, climbing and walking, country sports, chess and bridge, crafts, dogs, gardening, natural history, motoring.

● **Elliott Right Way Books**: how-to and instruction books on a wide range of subjects, including cookery, DIY, family finance and legal matters, family health and fitness, pets, popular education.

● **W Foulsham & Co**: most subjects, including astrology, cookery, gardening, business, hobbies, sport, health, marriage.

● **Hamlyn**: popular non-fiction, particularly cookery, gardening, craft, sport, film tie-ins, rock'n'roll.

● **How To Books Ltd**: books for everyone wishing to develop self-reliance, acquire new skills, prepare for new responsibilities, and achieve important personal goals. (The publishers of this book.)

● **Piatkus Books**: self-help, biography, personal growth, business and management, careers, cookery, health and beauty, popular psychology.

● **Thames and Hudson Ltd**: art, archaeology, architecture and design, biography, crafts, fashion, history, mythology, music, photography, popular culture, travel, topography... a huge range.

● **Thorsons**: self-improvement, health, cookery, medical, alternative medical, crafts and hobbies.

7
Writing Specialist Non-Fiction

THE RELIGIOUS PRESS

Magazines catering for all religious denominations need inspirational and educational material. Most of the religious publications in the UK are related to the Christian faith in its various denominations – *The Catholic Herald, The Tablet, New Christian Herald, Church Times* and many others. You'll find other religious publications listed in the *Writers' & Artists' Yearbook* and *The Writer's Handbook*, including several well-known Jewish publications like the *Jewish Chronicle* and the *Jewish Telegraph*. Many smaller religious groups publish their own papers and magazines. You're probably already familiar with the publications relating to your own faith, but you might not have thought of them as markets for your writing.

Whatever your religious persuasion, however, you should apply the same basic principles for successful writing: study each publication as an individual market, because they're all different and will look for material that satisfies their particular outlook and interests.

There's also a society for writers of specifically Christian material, **The Fellowship of Christian Writers**.

Some publishers of religious and theological books
- **Christian Focus Publications**: adult and children's Christianity, including some children's fiction.

- **T & T Clark**: religion, theology, law and philosophy, for academic and professional markets.

- **Darton, Longman & Todd Ltd**: predominantly Christian, with an emphasis on spirituality, the ministry and the Church's mission.

- **Epworth Press**: Christian books only, on philosophy, theology, biblical studies and social concern.

- **HarperCollins**: all denominations, coverage includes both popular and academic spirituality, music, reference, bibles, missals, prayer-books and hymn books.

- **Hodder & Stoughton Religious**: a wide range of Christian paperbacks.

- **Lion Publishing**: Christian books for all ages, many illustrated, for popular international reading.

Most cities and large towns have at least one religious bookshop. You can browse in these and look for the publishers whose books reflect your own religious interests. If you buy one or two, so much the better – you could then enlist the shop staff's help for advice about appropriate publishers. Your library, too, should have information on religious publications.

Books on writing for the religious press
Writer's Digest Books publish a book on religious writing, *Writing to Inspire* by William Gentz and Lee Roddy.
   Allison & Busby publish *How To Write for Religious Markets* by Brenda Courtie.

EDUCATIONAL WRITING

You don't have to be a teacher to write educational material. Teaching experience helps, certainly, in preparing course material or textbooks, but the most important requirement is skill in communication.
   The educational writer has to work within fairly strict guidelines. Content, language and structure must be geared to specific ages and abilities. You can get information on courses and required syllabus material from local education authorities, career centres and libraries. If you are a teacher you have an advantage over the 'outsider', because you're in touch with current needs.
   There are openings, however, for those with no teaching experience at all. What you need is the ability to write well to specific guidelines.

English language teaching
The English language is taught all over the world, not only to children but to people of all ages. Most of this teaching is done with

storybooks, not textbooks. Some of these are original stories, but many are adapted from modern novels and from the life stories of famous people – Marilyn Monroe, Charlie Chaplin, Winston Churchill... Non-fiction subjects like airports, animals, earthquakes, the sinking of the Titanic and the Olympic Games are popular, too.

What is required is a 'good read' to keep the learner turning the pages so that he absorbs the language almost without thinking about it. These abridgements and adaptations have to be prepared within tight disciplines according to varying levels of ability. At the lower level, for example, you might work with

- a given word list of, say, 300 words
- a given list of simple sentence structures
- very simple tenses.

With these as your basic 'bricks', you build a story or, for an adaptation, you use the existing storyline. You would be asked to work within specific wordage limits.

If you think you could make a go of this kind of tightly disciplined writing, contact publishers who have an English Language Teaching (ELT) department, citing any relevant qualifications and writing experience, and including any ideas you might have for stories or adaptations.

Reference books

These can be a good publishing proposition because they're steady sellers. There are reference books on every imaginable subject, from wildflowers to monastery sewerage systems. If you have an idea for a reference book – perhaps you've spotted a gap in the market – and have enough knowledge of the subject to write it, approach a publisher with a proposal as outlined in Chapter 6.

Some publishers of educational books
- Cambridge University Press
- Cassell
- HarperCollins
- Hodder & Stoughton
- Macmillan Education

And of reference books
- Cambridge University Press
- How To Books Ltd
- Macmillan Reference and Financial
- Kogan Page
- Oxford University Press.

There are many others – consult the *Writers' & Artists' Yearbook* and *The Writer's Handbook*.

TRAVEL WRITING

Successful travel writing involves much more than descriptions of journeys and exotic locations, or quoting from brochures and guide books. A travel article or book should:

- provide insight into the people's lives and culture
- create a sense of atmosphere
- bring a place to vivid life through details rather than generalities
- get the facts right, but treat them imaginatively
- be descriptive without being overloaded with superlatives, clichés and fulsome adjectives.

Too many aspiring travel writers concentrate on descriptions of beautiful sights seen through the windows of their car or tourist coach. You need to spend time absorbing the local atmosphere, talking to the people, taking photographs and making on-the-spot notes of your impressions – not just what you see, but what you feel, hear and smell, what attracts, what repels, what arouses your curiosity. Dig beneath the surface, and be sensitive to the implications of what you find.

If you need inspiration, don't turn to guides or brochures – read Jonathan Raban, Eric Newby, Jan Morris, Paul Theroux and the hugely successful Bill Bryson . . .the best travel writers can transport the armchair traveller into the heart of another place, another culture. They make you feel the thin air of the Andes, see the grandeur of the Victoria Falls, smell the sweat that built the Pyramids, hear the echo of the jackboot in the streets of Warsaw.

Travel writing has more in common with fiction than with journalism. It needs more than facts, figures and descriptions – it needs the pulse of life. If you can achieve this, you'll delight the editors who receive your mss.

Don't forget the photographs. They could be vital in clinching a sale.

Books to help you
- Morag Campbell, *Writing About Travel.*
- L Peat O'Neil, *Travel Writing.*

Some publishers of travel books
- Jonathan Cape Ltd
- Constable & Co Ltd
- Swan Hill Press (Airlife Publishing Co)
- Ian Allan Ltd
- How To Books Ltd

Magazines
Many general interest magazines publish travel articles. In most cases, you need to be able to offer something specific, focusing on an unusual aspect or region. Avoid areas that have already been done to death. Good photographs will help your writing sell.

Overseas magazines could be interested in pieces about the UK which is, of course, 'abroad' to all other countries.

TECHNICAL WRITING

To be a successful technical writer, you need many of the qualities and skills of an investigative journalist. You need to know how to sift essential information from masses of data, then represent that information in terms that are easily understood by the people who need it.

To be a technical writer, you would need:

- to enjoy researching, possibly into subject matter you know little or nothing about, in enough depth to clarify the subject to people who need to understand it

- to be skilled enough in human relationships to win co-operation from the people who hold the information you need – you might have to apply a little psychology when you deal with a temperamental genius (or even worse, with someone who thinks he's a genius)

- to possess a logical mind and a good memory

- to be able to present your findings in clear, concise, unambiguous English, without resort to specialist jargon.

It's that last point that prompts many businesses to employ writers from outside the company to prepare sales brochures, users' manuals and suchlike. Company employees can be too close to the subject to see that what is commonplace knowledge to them might be a complete mystery to the layman or non-technician. If you've ever torn your hair out over a computer handbook you'll recognise the problem. An 'outsider' sees the gaps and the areas of possible confusion because he needs to get them clear in his own mind before he can pass them on to his readers.

Technical Writing: City & Guilds
John Crossley is Principal of The College of Technical Authorship, which offers distance-learning courses leading to City & Guilds qualifications. John says, 'Employers look for consistent common sense, staying power, logic and persistence as well as writing ability. Achieving the City & Guilds Certificate in Technical Authorship provides ample evidence that you possess these qualities, and you will be able to show that the exams include practical tests of your writing ability.' John Crossley is a Member of the Institute of Scientific and Technical Communicators. He will send you details of his course on the two-part City & Guilds 'Tech 536' scheme on request. His address is on page 167.

COPYWRITING

Copywriting for business can be very lucrative. The main areas are advertising and direct mail. To get a feel for what's needed, stop skipping the adverts and binning your 'junk' mail. Somebody has been paid to write all that material, and paid very well. Maybe you could do it, too, and develop a useful sideline or even a new career writing copy designed to sell products and services.

You could start by offering your services to local companies. Study their promotional material. Could you write it better? Can you think up a more effective approach? If so, let them see it. Show them what you can do. Present fresh ideas, demonstrate sharp persuasive language.

As Kit Sadgrove says in his excellent book *Writing to Sell*, 'The language of advertising is different from the schoolroom.'

Whether you're writing press releases, adverts, sales literature, newsletters, posters or TV and radio commercials, you need to know how to construct good copy and avoid the pitfalls.

Your writing skills could help small businesses in particular to do this better and at less expense than could a large advertising company.

Recommended books
- Alastair Crompton, *The Craft of Copywriting*
- J Jonathan Gabay, *Teach Yourself Copywriting*
- Kit Sadgrove, *Writing to Sell* (Hale 1991 – out of print – worth finding).

8
Writing Short Stories

When we were planning an earlier edition of this book, we invited readers to complete a questionnaire that would give us information about the relative popularity of the various fields of writing. We intended, if necessary, to revise the content so we could give aspiring writers the information they really wanted. When we analysed the results we were not really surprised to find that short-story writing was the most enjoyed and the most widely practised of all the writing genres.

What did surprise us, however, was the extent of the short story's lead in the popularity stakes. It finished about 20 percentage points ahead of its nearest rival, the novel.

You might wonder why it is, then, that publishers find short story collections so difficult to sell, with the occasional exception of volumes of stories by authors who are either famous already or at least comparatively well known. The few brave souls who have launched magazines devoted to the short story have also failed to survive, having found the reading public unwilling to support their efforts by actually buying the publications rather than submitting manuscripts in the hope of seeing their own stories in print.

The situation is similar to that of poetry publishing. If every writer who wants to get their work published would go out and buy even one volume each year, both poetry and short story publishing would blossom and thrive.

As things are, the competition to get short stories published gets keener every year. To succeed, you need much more than talent and luck.

That said, however, the writer who is prepared to study the craft and the markets should not take too much notice of the many writers who complain that 'You can't sell short stories these days – editors don't want them...'.

Comments like that are almost invariably made by unsuccessful writers who don't – or won't – recognise the true situation. The popular magazines can't get enough short stories. Good short stories. Well written, entertaining, publishable short stories.

Editorial desks groan under dull, clichéd, sermonising stories, lifeless, formless, pointless stories, sad, sordid, despairing stories... Editors don't want them. Their readers don't want them.

In 1984, when *Woman's Own* decided to stop reading unsolicited fiction (the first British women's magazine to do so), editor Iris Burton told a writers' magazine that reading the hundreds of mss they received every year was highly time-consuming and almost totally non-productive. Since then, many other magazines have adopted this policy, for the same reasons. Good short fiction was 'as hard to come by as ever', Iris Burton said, but far too few writers really study the market, and to be commercially successful a writer must combine creativity with pragmatism. She had to buy much of their fiction from America, where writers take a much more professional and analytical approach.

There you have it, the key to writing successful, saleable short stories: *a professional and analytical approach.*

WRITING STORIES THAT SELL

A saleable short story needs a structure (beginning, middle, end), a theme, a plot, sound syntax and grammar, and language appropriate to its subject and to its intended market.

You can learn how to do it. There are classes and seminars, courses and books that specialise in short-story writing. You can read, study and analyse published short stories by past and contemporary writers.

Let's look at some aspects of fiction-writing that seem to trouble new writers in particular.

Finding plots

Every plot begins with an idea. And ideas are everywhere. They're all around you – and inside you, too. Fantasy novelist Ursula le Guin, quoted in the American magazine *The Writer* (October 1991) says that when she's asked where she gets her ideas, she replies: 'I don't get them, I am them: a writer's life is her ideas, her work, her words.'

Try this: every day for a week, read your daily and Sunday newspapers from cover to cover (advertisements and all) and clip out every item that arouses even the mildest interest. Letters to the editor, the life-style sections, reviews, financial and sports pages as well as news stories – skip nothing. Collect anything that intrigues.

Browse through your cuttings, and let your imagination run

free... What made that young girl so desperate that she left an apparently happy and comfortable home to live rough on city streets? Why did that householder go to such lengths to prevent his neighbour uprooting a dying section of their commonly-owned hedge? How did that woman fare when she returned to her job after winning her case for unfair dismissal? Would being 'Slimmer of the Year' change a man's life more than it would a woman's? What if... and if...?

Beware plot 'formulae'. 'Dial-a-Plot' or 'The Miracle Plot Menu' might seem to offer an easy route to brilliantly plotted stories, but in fact they're a waste of time and money. Good plots stem from the actions, reactions and interactions of characters, not from any artificial recipes or manipulation of events. You want something that's uniquely yours, not some stale, clichéd, over-used plot that will make the editor groan 'Oh no, not that one again!'

Keep a notebook with you at all times – the germ of a really original plot might bubble up in your brain at the most unexpected moment. Don't lose it.

Viewpoint

This is simply the point of view from which the story is told. This might be through the eyes of the hero or heroine or any other character, in first person or third person, or by an 'omniscient' storyteller who sees and hears everything.

It's a useful exercise to take one of your stories and write it several times, from the viewpoints of different characters. Does the story work better from any particular viewpoint? Is it more convincing? More intriguing? More exciting? Can you analyse why?

Some stories almost demand to be told from several different viewpoints. This is more likely with novels than with short stories, though, as there is usually less scope for jumping from one character's mind to another's within the limited action and wordage of the short story. If you do decide on the multiple viewpoint, avoid changing viewpoints within a scene. This can diffuse the impact, and might confuse or irritate the reader.

For the beginner, it's probably best to tell your story from the viewpoint of a single lead character. This will help to hold your story together by giving it a stronger emotional focus.

Then you need to decide whether first person or third person narrative would serve your story best. This is often simply a matter of taste and suitability. Try both ways, to see which works best for your story. If you opt for first person, don't fall into the trap of 'The

Big I Syndrome', where hardly a line is written without the use of 'I', 'me', 'myself' or 'mine'. This ineptitude ruins many first-person stories and makes even a potentially exciting story boring and repetitive. Take a highlighter pen and mark every use of 'I' and so on – you'll soon see if you've used too many.

BEING YOUR OWN EDITOR

Don't shy away from revising and rewriting – your words aren't chiselled in stone, and self-criticism is a valuable skill to acquire. It pays to be ruthless at this stage, however painful you find it. These are some of the faults and weaknesses likely to affect an editor's decision:

1. Is the **opening** too long? Too slow? Too general? It's vital to grip the reader's interest, curiosity and emotions right away.

2. Have you **begun** in the right place? Begin at an intriguing point in the action. You can filter in information about previous events as the story progresses.

3. Is there too much **flashback**? Too much scene-setting through characters' memories can kill the story's pace.

4. Are your **characters** fully developed, and portrayed through their actions, reactions and interactions rather than by bald exposition?

5. Have you maintained **momentum** through the middle section, moving the story forward through cause and effect, building towards the **climax**? Or have you cluttered the narrative with unnecessary detail and superfluous characters? (Seeing an old woman begging in the street might remind your hero of his good fortune despite his present troubles, but we don't need to know how Betty the Baglady came to fall on hard times.) Keep the focus where it belongs.

6. Is the **ending** satisfying, believable, and logical in the story's own terms? Or did you run out of steam, leave unintentional loose ends, or cheat your reader with a contrived 'twist' or a hitherto unseen character who appears with all the answers (the classic *deus ex machina*)?

7. Is the **viewpoint** consistent? The tiniest shift can destroy the reader's empathy. For example, your hero sees his lost love: 'David felt his heart thump, and tears began to sting his blue eyes...' The single word 'blue' takes us from inside David's mind and asks us to observe him from outside, making us look at him rather than feel with him.

8. Have you chosen suitable **names**? Inappropriate names could 'place' characters in age bands or social categories different from those you intended: 'Ada and Herbert', 'Tracey and Kev', 'Lucinda and Peregrine' evoke different perceptions and expectations.

9. Is the **dialogue** natural? Or does it seem stilted and unconvincing? Read it aloud, tape it if possible, and listen for awkward phrases and out-of-character speech patterns and vocabulary. Use abbreviations – 'couldn't', 'he'd', 'they'll' and so on – where they feel right.

10. Have you allowed the reader to use his **imagination**? Or have you described every move, every thought, every feeling? We don't need to know every little detail. Leave some gaps for your reader to fill in. Don't be afraid of time and scene 'jumps'. This will help give pace to your story, too.

11. Is your **spelling** sound? Careless spelling can alter or fog your meaning – and it gives the editor negative messages about you as a writer.

12. And your **punctuation**? Inaccurate punctuation can produce nonsense: 'The rain was pouring down Carol' doesn't mean the same as 'The rain was pouring down, Carol'.

13. And your **syntax**? Syntax is the ordering of words to convey a clear and unambiguous meaning. Consider this: 'The mayor arrived to light the bonfire with his wife.' All the right words are there, but their order makes the statement absurd. Make sure you've actually said what you intended to say.

14. Are your **tenses** consistent? It's all too easy to shift from present to past and vice versa without noticing.

15. Is your writing **concise and sharp**? Or wordy and slack? The more compact your prose, the stronger its impact. Especially avoid weak verbs that need adverbs to reinforce their meaning: a branch *fell heavily* to the ground – try *thudded*.

16. Have you used *active* rather than *passive* **verbs**? 'Fido chased Felix' is stronger than 'Felix was chased by Fido'.

17. Have you avoided **vagueness**? 'There was quite a crowd waiting to see the parade' is woolly – try to be more specific: 'Crowds waited ten-deep along the parade route.'

18. Is your text **repetitive**? Don't bore your reader with 'Mary's mother said this' and 'Mary's mother said that', 'Suddenly this' and 'Suddenly that'... Vary your vocabulary.

FINDING MARKETS

Let's look at just a few, to give you a start. Then you must dig them out for yourself, from your newsagent's shelves (make friends with him first), from writers' magazines, the *Writers' & Artists' Yearbook*, *The Writer's Handbook*, *Writers' Bulletin*. Keep up with new publications as they appear on the stands.

Don't just look at the obvious markets. Search among the specialist and hobby publications – some of these will consider short fiction that's directly relevant to their areas of interest. Some regional magazines and newspapers, too, publish short stories.

The popular women's magazines

You don't have to be a woman to write for women's and family magazines. You don't even have to write 'women's' stories. The weekly magazines *Best* and *Bella* each publish one short-short story and one longer short story in every issue. That means slots for 208 stories every year just in these two magazines. *Take a Break* and *Chat* publish 'twist-in-the-tail' stories, 800-1,000 words.

Some women's magazines prefer male writers to adopt a feminine pen-name, but more and more masculine bylines are appearing.

Publishers D C Thomson & Co Ltd are very helpful to promising new writers. They're always interested in writers who can supply the right kind of fiction for their publications, which include *My Weekly* and *People's Friend*. As well as short stories, they need serial stories for the weekly magazines, and short romantic or romantic-suspense novels, 35-40,000 words long, for My Weekly Story Library.

D C Thomson are always in the market to find good new writers for their wide range of publications, as shown by the many different leaflets we provide.
New writers have to face the fact that competition for success is fierce. Because of the volume of contributions received, encouragement to new writers from editors can only go to those who show most promise in producing our kind of material.
Once you have studied the market, send your story to the editor of the magazine at which it is aimed or to the Central Fiction Department which acts as a clearing-house for unsolicited contributions.

The Fiction Editor, D C Thomson & Co Ltd

Note the phrases: 'our kind of material' and 'once you have studied the market'. You have to show not only better than average writing ability, but also an awareness of the company's needs. They offer encouragement and advice, not tuition in writing.

D C Thomson will send you their guidelines on request. These leaflets include writing for their women's magazines and for My Weekly Story Library. They also have leaflets available on writing children's and teenage picture- and photo-story scripts, and will send you details of how to submit your mss.

Agency
Midland Exposure Agency (Cari Crook and Lesley Gleeson) will assess your short stories with a view to offering them in the market (see page 167).

Small press magazines
There are dozens of small press magazines publishing short stories, and this is where many writers get their foot on the first rung of the publishing ladder. The small presses pay very little, and often only pay in copies of the magazine, but competition for publication here is still fiercely contested and, in the main, standards are high. A few of these are:

- *Acumen*, editor Patricia Oxley. Includes original short stories.

- *Stand*, editors Jon Silkin and Lorna Tracy. Includes original short fiction, embracing experimental and sometimes controversial work. They run an annual short story competition which is regarded as one of the most prestigious to win.

- *QWF (Quality Women's Fiction)*, editor Jo Good. A showcase for women's original short stories.

- *Peninsular* and *Writers' Express*, both from Cherrybite Publications, editor Shelagh Nugent. Both magazines include original short fiction.

- *Writers' Own Magazine*, editor Eileen M Pickering. Includes original short fiction.

- *The Deansgate Portfolio (Alien Landings)*. A showcase for quality short fiction in the science fiction, fantasy and horror genres. Edited by 'Ariel' and Paul Wake and published under the wing of Waterstones, Deansgate, Manchester. Send an SAE for submission guidelines.

You should always study at least one issue of a magazine before you send any work to it, to familiarise yourself with its style and flavour. Not every magazine, of course, will suit your style, and you don't want to waste either your time and money (or theirs) on unsuitable work.

Most magazines will sell you a single copy on request, but please don't ask or expect them to hand out free copies. These are small businesses often struggling to survive, and they can't afford to subsidise your market study. Remember, too, always to enclose an SAE for a reply to any query.

BOOKS TO HELP YOU

- *Creating a Twist in the Tale*, by Adele Ramet. How to write popular, short, twist-ending stories widely published in women's magazines, by a highly successful writer of the genre.

- *How to Write a Miffion*, by Dibell, Scott Card and Turco. The best three titles of the 'Writers' Workshop' series in a single volume. Great value, great advice. If you can only afford one book on writing fiction to begin with, make this the one. The wisdom in these pages applies to all kinds of fiction-writing.

- *The Complete Guide to Writing Fiction*, by Barnaby Conrad and the staff of Santa Barbara Writers' Conference. Practical, helpful, inspiring, and all the superlatives you can think of. A really good guide covering every aspect of fiction writing, with contributions from the giants: Ray Bradbury, Judith Krantz, Sidney Sheldon, Martin Cruz Smith, Joseph Wambaugh...

- *How to Write Short-Short Stories* by Stella Whitelaw. How to write one-page 'coffee-break' fiction for popular magazines.

A few publishers of volumes of short stories
(Don't submit single stories. Wait till you can put together a collection which, preferably, includes at least a few that have been published in magazines.)

- Bloomsbury
- Jonathan Cape
- Serpent's Tail
- Faber & Faber
- Viking
- Vintage

And he didn't have to wait till he was President
Everybody, it seems, wants to publish a short story. Abraham Lincoln had his published in the Quincy, Illinois, *Whig* of 15 April 1846. *The Trailor Murder Mystery*, based on a true case, was reprinted in the March 1952 issue of *Ellery Queen's Mystery Magazine*.

9
Writing Your First Novel

GETTING IT RIGHT

Publishers will heap blessings on your head if you can offer an original novel that's in tune with today's markets – better still, tomorrow's.

It can take two or three years to bring a novel from its first assessment to its appearance in the bookshops. Publishers have to be forward-thinking. So does the smart writer. It's a waste of time trying to catch the coat-tails of today's bestsellers.

The nearest you'll get to a crystal ball is to read the weekly trade magazine *The Bookseller*, especially the fat Spring and Autumn numbers, each of which has about 800 pages of news and information about what is in the pipeline for the coming six months. These special issues are far from cheap, but if you've made a friend of your local bookseller (and you should) he might let you browse through his copy. The weekly *Publishing News* is helpful, too.

How a success story began
Robert Goddard began his first novel in May 1983, with a rough draft of the plot. Then over the next six months or so he put together notes, mostly from his own experience, until he had a 30-page summary of the projected novel. And he began to write.

He completed the first 50 pages and sent them to publishers Robert Hale, whom a friend had recommended. They were interested enough to ask to see the complete novel. It was finished in January 1985. Then came almost a year of assessment followed by lengthy negotiations about cutting the overlong ms, before the contract was signed.

Robert was delighted and amazed that his first novel had been accepted by the first publisher he tried. *Past Caring* was published in 1986. It's a gripping story in which political and personal intrigue reach out from the early years of the century to ensnare characters of the present day. Its publishers regarded it so highly they nominated it for the Booker Prize.

Plan your novel thoroughly from beginning to end. Then write 50 or 60 pages of it. Invest in those pages as much energy, creativity and conviction as you can summon. Type them accurately. Package them attractively. Then try them on a publisher or agent. If there is real merit in them it will be recognised.

Robert Goddard

Since that initial success, Robert Goddard has published a new novel every year, and they've all been successful sellers in both hardback and paperback. The paperback of his fourth novel, *Into the Blue*, won the first-ever W H Smith 'Thumping Good Read' Award, in 1992.

BOOKS TO HELP YOU

* Lawrence Block, *Writing the Novel from Plot to Print.* A very readable guide to success from an American writer with more than 100 published novels to his credit. Lawrence Block also wrote the 'Fiction-writing' column in *Writer's Digest* magazine for many years.

* John Braine, *Writing a Novel.* A thoroughly practical exposition of the novelist's craft, regarded as a classic on the subject.

* Marina Oliver, *Writing & Selling a Novel.* Expert guidance from a writer who has published over 30 novels.

* Jean Saunders, *How to Create Fictional Characters* and *How to Write Realistic Dialogue.* Step-by-step guidance from a highly successful novelist.

* Michael Legat, *Writing for Pleasure and Profit.* This excellent all-rounder is particularly good on novel-writing.

* Gary Provost, *Make Every Word Court.* A detailed analysis of how to write richly textured yet concise narrative and dialogue.

* Phyllis Whitney, *Guide to Fiction Writing.* One of the most popular writers of romantic-suspense fiction tells you how it's done.

• Celia Brayfield, *Bestseller*. Insight, inspiration and motivation, combined with a thoughtful and penetrating analysis of the craft of novel-writing.

• Gordon Wells, *The Book Writer's Handbook*. Useful both as a market guide for the first-time novelist and as a reference for established authors seeking new outlets. Look for the latest edition. You need the most up-to-date information available in today's volatile publishing world.

WRITING 'GENRE' FICTION

In most of the writers' manuals you'll read, you'll see references to 'genre' or 'category' fiction. Some 'literary' writers and critics use these terms in a derogatory way, but don't let that worry you. It's no more and no less difficult to write a good 'genre' novel than it is to write a good 'general' novel. Publishers divide novels into 'categories' simply for ease of reference. Bear in mind, too, that the categories frequently overlap: 'romantic-suspense', 'spy-thriller', 'war-adventure' and so on. You can combine them as you wish.

How could you categorise, for instance, Douglas Adams's *Dirk Gently's Holistic Detective Agency*? *The Bookseller* defined it as 'Ghost-Horror-Detective-Whodunnit-Time-Travel-Romantic-Musical-Comedy'.

Crime and mystery

Most of the major publishers have crime lists, and they'll snap up a good original story, especially if you can create a character or characters who could be developed for a series of books. H R F Keating's 'Inspector Ghote', Ruth Rendell's 'Wexford', Reginald Hill's 'Dalziel and Pascoe', Jonathan Gash's 'Lovejoy', Colin Dexter's 'Morse'...their sales go up with every new story.

To write modern crime stories successfully, you have to keep up to date with developments in detection methods – genetic fingerprinting, for instance, and computerised databanks. You can't afford to get left behind, or to make mistakes. Crime story mss are assessed by experts who will spot any errors or clumsy fudging. Don't risk your credibility by neglecting your research.

On the other hand, don't be so earnest you forget you're writing a story that people will read for relaxation and entertainment. You're not in the business of writing forensic textbooks.

The more I come to think of it the more I come to believe the key to successful fiction writing is always, on every page, with every word, to tell it to your readers. It's what all the great writers did; it's what all the bestselling writers do. Do it too.

H R F Keating

H R F Keating has been writing successful crime stories since the 1960s. He also writes what he calls 'mystery with history', crime novels in a Victorian setting, under the pen-name of Evelyn Hervey. In his book *Writing Crime Fiction* he shares his experience and knowledge of crime writing and crime novels. His advice and insights on writing will be invaluable to all fiction writers, whatever their preferred genre.

In *Plotting and Writing Suspense Fiction*, Patricia Highsmith discusses her own experience of writing, charting her failures as well as her successes. She claims that the book 'is not a how-to-do-it' handbook, but in fact it's packed with detailed analyses of the techniques of mystery-suspense writing.

And no crime-writer's bookshelf is complete without Julian Symon's *Bloody Murder*, a history of crime-writing from its beginning to the early 1980s.

Crime and passion

Virgin Publishing recently launched a new cross-genre imprint 'Crime & Passion', which combines crime fiction and erotic fiction. All the stories are written around characters already formulated by the publishers. Fully comprehensive and detailed guidelines are available from the publisher, Peter Darvill-Evans. The address is given under 'More Useful Addresses' in the appendices.

Thrills and spies

Thrillers of all kinds are big sellers. Wilbur Smith, Robert Ludlum, Dick Francis... their books shoot straight into the bestseller lists.

Fast-moving, visual writing works best. Television has conditioned thriller addicts to expect plenty of action. The long descriptive passages that used to be essential for scene-setting bore today's readers, whose memories hold a huge storehouse of images. They don't need descriptions of a crocodile, a computer, Red Square or the pyramids. And they're used to cutting from scene to scene.

Spy stories have become highly sophisticated, and the writing's better, too. The reading public's knowledge of computer-hacking for

information, 'spy-in-the-sky' satellites and psychiatric drugs makes
Ian Fleming's early James Bond 'fairy-tales-with-gadgets' seem as
unreal as Thunderbirds. We've grown weary, too, of Le Carré-type
'seedy mutterings in dingy corridors somewhere off the Charing
Cross Road'. Glasnost and the demolition of the Berlin Wall, so
swiftly followed by the break-up of the Soviet Union, have changed
the focus of spy stories for the foreseeable future. Sharp writers
moved at once to a new centre of interest. Check the bookshop
shelves – note how many stories now focus on the Middle East,
reviving the centuries-old differences between the West and Islam.

Some publishers with strong crime and thriller lists
Constable, Gollancz, HarperCollins, Headline, Macmillan, Little,
Brown, Arrow. The Women's Press publishes feminist crime and
thrillers. Espionage is published by Hodder Headline, HarperCollins, Century.

Action-adventure
Easy to recognise, but almost impossible to define, an action-
adventure story can be set anywhere in the world, in the present or
in the past, even in the future, where it crosses boundaries into
science fiction.

Fast-moving, full of action and excitement, with plenty of cliff-
hangers – these are the essentials. You need to create dynamic
characters, fleshed-out and convincing enough to make your reader
believe in them for the duration of the story.

Some publishers of action-adventure
Bantam Press, HarperCollins, Hodder & Stoughton, Little, Brown.

Westerns
The Western is a clearly definable genre. According to the Western
Writers of America, it's a story set West of the Mississippi River
before the 20th century.

Like popular romantic fiction, the Western is unjustly regarded
with disdain by 'literary' authors and editors. J T Edson is an
Englishman who has made a hugely successful career writing
Westerns. J T is a passionate champion of the genre, and is an
authority on the history of the old West.

He says he feels he should warn aspiring writers of Westerns that
he finds editorial staff have been conditioned from early childhood
to regard the genre as substandard literature. They're disinclined to

believe that an author who specialises in Westerns can possibly write anything else which will prove saleable. If you write, as J T does, under your own name, you might find it hard to be taken seriously should you want to break into another genre. You could try Robert Hale, but you might have to send your mss to publishers in the United States. Consult the American *Writer's Market*.

Science fiction, fantasy and horror

From H G Wells to Ray Bradbury, some of the most exciting writing in English literature explores the possibilities of life and intelligence beyond the known frontiers of time and space. Good writers who can supply what the science fiction market needs will be welcomed with open cheque books.

Don't be tempted to think of fantasy and horror as a 'hack' market, either. In an article published in 1973 in the American *Writer's Digest*, Stephen King described the genre as 'one of the most delicate known to man and it must be handled with great care and more than a little love'.

Within the accepted rules of good story-telling (that a story should be original, gripping and well crafted) there are no restrictions. You can make magic, you can set your tale anywhere, anytime, in this world or in one of your own making. The *Lord of the Rings* is a fantasy. So is *Superman*.

But remember that a successful fantasy needs its own disciplines. It should be logical within its own terms. And above all it should tell a story. Enchanted lands, elves, monsters, mystery and magic are only elements of a story, not a substitute for it.

If you lean towards the horror side of fantasy, and enjoy reading Stephen King, Brian Lumley, Dean R Koontz and James Herbert – in other words, if you enjoy having your blood curdled – you'll realise that the most successful horror writers play on our own fears: fear of the dark, of death, of private personal horrors like rats, bats, snakes and spiders, but most of all on our fear of the unknown.

It's an intensely personal genre. To succeed, you need total faith in what you're writing.

Don't always listen to editors, and never listen to friends. A very small number of my works were improved by the suggestions of editors, but just as many have been damaged. Don't deliberately shape your work to another's design; if it's not quite right just now, come back to it when your inner man (woman) has had time to solve the problems. Remember: the road to many a moderate literary success is thick with the ghosts of friendly advice and the dust of dead friendships.

Brian Lumley

Books to help you
- Christopher Kenworthy, *Writing Science Fiction, Fantasy and Horror*. Demystifies the art and turns ideas into stories that sell, using exercises, questionnaires and checklists.

- Ben Bova, *The Craft of Writing Science Fiction That Sells*. Covers all aspects of the genre, and shows how to write original dynamic stories that sell.

Some publishers of science fiction, fantasy and horror
Orbit (Little, Brown), Macmillan, Legend (Random House), Robinson, Gollancz, New English Library.

Romance, romantic-suspense, romantic-historical
Don't skip this bit just because you're a man. Romantic novelists 'Jennifer Wilde' and 'Vanessa Royall' are both men, and Mills & Boon (now known as Harlequin, Mills & Boon) have at least two men among their regular writers. Mills & Boon Reader Service offers detailed guidelines and an audio cassette.

In 1996 Robinson Publishing launched their new romantic fiction imprint 'Scarlet', which offers its readers 'sexy, humorous, adventurous, fast-paced, emotionally intense contemporary romances' written by both established and new writers. Guidelines are available on request.

The Romantic Novelists' Association offers membership on a probationary basis, even if you've had nothing published yet.

Some books to help you
- Mary Wibberley, *To Writers With Love*. Entertaining and challenging, guaranteed to get you writing. Mary has specialised in writing for Mills & Boon, and her book is especially useful in its insights into that particular publisher's requirements. She now also writes for Robinson Publishing's 'Scarlet' imprint.

- Jean Saunders, *The Craft of Writing Romance*. Covers a wide range of romantic writing, with enlightening contributions from editors and successful writers in the genre.

- Valerie Parv, *The Art of Romance Writing*. Mainly intended for would-be Mills & Boon authors, but a valuable addition to any romance writer's bookshelf. Gives useful insights into motivation and behaviour (with leads to further reading) to help achieve depth and texture in writing about human relationships.

- Marina Oliver, *Writing Romantic Fiction*. Pinpoints the special skills and qualities needed to succeed in this best-selling genre.

And when you're ready, **a few publishers to try**: HarperCollins, Piatkus Books, Transworld Publishers, Hodder Headline, Little, Brown.

Erotic fiction
Publishers with 'erotic fiction' lists are keen to find writers for this genre, which has become a highly profitable seller in recent years. Writers who can tell a good story with the emphasis on erotic (not pornographic) sex are hard to find, it seems.

Comprehensive guidelines are available from Virgin's Black Lace imprint, where a million and a half copies were sold in the first two years of publishing. Black Lace publishes 'erotic fiction written by women for women'. They say that the fact that all their writers are guaranteed to be women is an important part of their marketing strategy.

Following the success of Black Lace, other publishers have followed Virgin and launched erotic fiction imprints of their own. There's a golden opportunity here for writers who can supply what these publishers want.

Books to help you
- Derek Parker, *Writing Erotic Fiction*. The author of 15 erotic novels and two non-fiction books on eroticism in literature explains the genre and shows you how to write for it.

- Michael Rowe, *Writing Below the Belt*. Conversations with 15 authors of erotic literature reveal how the genre works.

Some publishers of erotic fiction
Black Lace (Virgin), Ex Libris (Little, Brown), Headline Delta Liaison (Hodder Headline).

10
Writing for Children and Teenagers

Do you have a fund of ideas for stories, informative articles, games, puzzles, jokes and picture-stories? There's plenty of room in the market for all of these – if you can write them really well.

WRITING CHILDREN'S BOOKS

Writing for children is a very specialised business. Don't make the mistake, as so many writers do, of assuming that it's easier to write for children than for adults. It isn't. You have to study the markets very closely, and work at developing the right kind of writing techniques. And those techniques will be different for each age group.

There's no room for amateur attitudes here. Publishers receive shoals of stories with enthusiastic covering letters assuring them 'My children loved this when I read it to them – I'm sure others will, too.' Many of these mss arrive complete with unbelievably bad illustrations ('My friend has kindly done the pictures for you. She's always been good at drawing'). Unless your collaborator's work is up to professional standard, this will kill your hopes of publication stone dead. Publishers usually prefer to commission illustrations from a regular 'stable' of artists whose work is of a type and standard that the publisher knows and trusts.

Writing and illustrating a story call for professional skills far beyond the ability to entertain your own or your neighbour's children, but if you think you'd like to investigate the possibility, read *How to Write & Illustrate Children's Books*, edited by Treld Pelkey Bicknell and Felicity Trotman.

The success rate in writing for children indicates that the younger the age group, the harder it is to cater for. The more simple and spare the writing, the more skill is needed to get it just right. When you read books on the subject by successful children's writers, you'll see what a complex discipline it is. Three of the best are *The Way to Write for Children* by Joan Aiken, *Writing for Young Children* by Claudia Lewis, and *How to Write for Children* by Tessa Krailing.

Read these, then decide if you could produce the kind of material publishers want. Some teachers believe that many publishers don't really know what children like to read. They could be right, but the writer who wants to get his or her children's book accepted by a publisher has to deliver what that publisher wants. (If you want to pioneer a revolution in children's books you'll probably have to become a publisher yourself.)

It's vital to study current markets. Many writers, especially older ones, tend to submit the kind of stories that were popular when their children (or even they themselves) were young. Their subject matter, language and treatment are out of touch with today's market.

Spend time in the children's section of the library, and look at recently published books, both fiction and non-fiction. Study the various age ranges – note how the vocabulary becomes more challenging as the target age increases. Note the subject matter and treatment.

Don't send work to any publisher without first making a detailed study of their products in the age range and type of book you want to write. Every publishing house strives for a distinct personality and style. Buy some of their books, get out your coloured pens, and analyse them down to the last comma. A vague notion of what the publisher wants will not be good enough.

Some publishers of children's books

Brimax Books, Heinemann Young Books, Methuen Children's Books (all now under the umbrella of Reed Books), Andersen Press, A & C Black, Child's Play (International) Ltd, HarperCollins, Dorling Kindersley, Scholastic, Walker Books.

You'll find many more listed in the *Writers' & Artists' Yearbook* and *The Writer's Handbook*. *The Bookseller* and *Publishing News* will keep you informed about what's being published.

If you can get in at the start when publishers launch a new imprint, you'll be ahead of the game. It always pays to keep your market research up to date.

Games, puzzles, jokes, comic strips

Many puzzle books and comics use freelance material. Look, for example, at D C Thomson's *The Dandy*, *The Beano*, *Twinkle*, *Mandy & Judy (M&J)*. Spend time studying the markets. There's a pretty fast turnover in new titles – not many achieve the long-term popularity of the old favourites, but it can pay to get in early when a new one appears. Up-to-the-minute ideas are always welcome.

Almost every newspaper and magazine uses comic strips. If you could think up another 'Dilbert' you'd make a fortune. There's also a hungry market for puzzles of all kinds. You can usually find names and addresses inside the puzzle magazines themselves.

Books to help you
How to Draw and Sell Comic Strips, by Alan McKenzie.
How to Compile and Sell Crosswords and Other Puzzles, by Graham R Stevenson.

WRITING FOR TEENAGERS

There's been a fast growth in this area over the last few years, with house after house launching new imprints to cater for the 'young adult' market. There are great opportunities here for the writer who can tune in to the adolescent and teenage wavelengths. You need to be able to write with understanding but without any hint of condescension, condemnation or preaching. You need to like young people. If today's teenagers horrify, disgust or alarm you, if you regard them as alien beings, it's probably best not to try.

Subject matter

Don't shy away from controversial topics. Whether from their own experience or that of their friends, most young people today can identify with such problems as a divorce or death in the family, single parenthood, homelessness, living rough, the 'generation gap', personal relationships, unemployment, shyness, trying to make sense of the adult world... Treated with sensitivity, stories about the problems of daily life as well as traumatic situations can help young adults to understand and come to terms with the darkest aspects of life.

Tessa Krailing's book *How to Write for Children*, mentioned earlier, gives sound advice and perceptive analysis of the problems involved. Jean Saunders includes a constructive chapter on writing for teenagers in her book *Writing Step by Step*. There are also two excellent books from A & C Black, *Writing for Children* by Margaret Clark and *Writing for the Teenage Market* by Ann de Gale.

Who publishes teenage books?

You'll find the most up-to-date information in *The Bookseller* and in *Publishing News*. The on-going volatile state of the publishing industry makes it absolutely vital to keep track of who has merged with whom, who has launched a new imprint, who looks like going out of business... Haunt your library and bookshops, check what is currently on the market. Look at the publishers' names, and note those who publish material that appeals to you. Note, too, the dates of first publication. You don't want to study styles, attitudes and 'in' language that have been 'out' for years.

A few publishers of 'young adult' fiction
Faber & Faber, Livewire (The Women's Press), Macmillan, Methuen, Penguin, Red Fox (Random House), Heinemann Young Books (Reed), Scholastic.

CRAFTING PICTURE-SCRIPTS

Picture stories are stories told in picture form, either drawn or using photographs. The illustrations incorporate text in the form of dialogue in 'balloons', and sometimes in captions in or below the pictures.

D C Thomson & Co Ltd are prolific publishers of picture-script magazines for boys and girls of all ages from pre-school to teenagers. They will send you, on request, a comprehensive pack of information about writing story scripts, and will encourage and advise you if you show promise in writing the right kind of material for them. Send for the guidelines and study them, then study the publications before you send in any material. Every magazine has its own distinctive characteristics, and you'll need to show an awareness of the specific requirements of any you choose to write for. Stories are not interchangeable among the magazines.

You won't be required to supply the illustrations – these are done by commissioned artists – but you must present your script in such a way that the artist has a clear idea of what you want your readers to see in each picture.

The sample script (Figure 13) shows you how this is done. It's the title page of a story from one of D C Thomson's girls' papers. You'll see that the speeches have to be very concise. There's no room in the pictures for long explanatory speeches. The text and illustrations work together to move the story along. And don't lose sight of the fact that what you're writing is a story, not just a series of scenes.

1 – Large heading picture. Leave space for title and the following introductory paragraph –

When Gary and Lesley Stark were orphaned in a road accident, they went to live at Springbank Children's Home.

Gary and Lesley hoped to find a foster family where they could remain together, but had been disappointed so far. One day, Mrs Martin, the house mother, had news of a young couple who wanted to foster the twins –

Picture shows Mrs Martin talking to the twins in her sitting room.

Mrs Martin – *Mr and Mrs Hardy seem a really nice young couple. They love children, but they haven't any of their own, so they'd like you to spend a weekend with them.*

Lesley – *That sounds terrific, Mrs Martin, but Gary and I won't build up our hopes too high. We've had a few disappointments already.*

2 – Caption – *But at first, the Hardys did seem to be the perfect foster parents* – Picture shows Mr and Mrs Hardy, a bright looking couple in their 30s, smiling as they lead the children from their car up the path to a small, neat terrace house with pretty front garden.

Mr Hardy – *We've been really looking forward to this weekend, kids! I hope you like our little house. It's going to be a bit of a tight fit with four people in it, but WE don't mind if YOU don't.*

Lesley – *It looks lovely, Mr Hardy, and we LIKE small houses – they're cosy!*

3 – Caption – *Mrs Hardy showed Lesley where she was going to sleep* – Picture shows Lesley looking puzzled as she looks around small room with nursery furniture in it. The room has clearly been meant for a baby.

Lesley – *Mrs Martin didn't tell me that you had a baby, Mrs Hardy. This room is a nursery, isn't it?*

Fig. 13. A sample script.
Reproduced by permission of D C Thomson & Co Ltd.
© D C Thomson & Co Ltd.

Mrs Hardy – *Yes it is, Lesley. We did have a little baby of our own years ago, but she died, soon after she was born. We haven't had the heart to change the room since.*

4 – Picture shows close-up of Lesley looking thoughtful.
Lesley – *Poor Mrs Hardy. It must have been terrible for her, to lose her baby like that. Let's hope Gary and I will be able to help her forget her sadness.*

5 – Caption – *At tea time –*
Picture shows Mrs Hardy serving twins boiled eggs, toast strips and glasses of milk. She and her husband have meat and salad and teapot set in front of them. Lesley is sitting next to Gary, glowering at him.
Mrs Hardy – *Here we are, kiddies – nice eggies with toast soldiers, and lovely milk. If you're good, there will be stewed apple for afterwards.*
Gary – *What! B-but...oww!*

6 – Picture shows Lesley smiling sweetly at her cross brother.
Gary – *You kicked me, Les. Watch where you're putting your feet.*
Lesley – *Sorry, Gary.*
(Thinks) – *I had to stop him complaining about the baby food Mrs Hardy has made for us.*

7 – *After tea*
Picture shows Gary and Lesley sitting in living room. The Hardys can be seen washing-up in kitchen through serving hatch.
Gary – *Why did they make that special baby tea for us, when they were having ham salad, Les? Do you think they were trying to save money?*
Lesley – *I expect they thought they were doing us a favour by making us a special meal. Maybe they don't realise ten-year-olds eat the same sort of food as grown ups.*

Fig. 13. A sample script (continued).

FINDING CORRESPONDENCE COURSES

There are specialised correspondence courses in writing for children:

- **The Academy of Children's Writers** offers a tutored course, with written assignments. You can examine the complete printed course material before you commit yourself.

- **The London School of Journalism** offers a tutored course, 'Writing for Children'.

- **The Writers' Advice Centre** offers courses, workshops, critiques, talks, writers' holidays.

The above organisations will send you details and current terms on request. The addresses are in the appendices under **Correspondence Courses**, page 167.

11
Writing Poetry, Song Lyrics and Greeting Cards

POETRY

Poetry – the Olympic Games of writing. There's no money in it, unless you're lucky enough to win a big competition, yet the battle for publication and recognition is at its most intense here. To take just one poetry magazine, *Outposts Poetry Quarterly* receives over 80,000 unsolicited poems every year. There's only space for 50 or so in each issue, but that doesn't stop them flooding in.

Getting started

How do you publish your poetry? Where do you start? Firstly you read other people's poetry – both contemporary and classical – sufficient to familiarise yourself with the art so that you know what you are doing. Then research the market – buy poetry books, subscribe to literary magazines. Get a clear picture in your mind of the contemporary scene, and support it, it is the one you wish to join. Finally send some of your own material off for consideration. Always typed and never without a stamped addressed envelope.

Peter Finch

Peter Finch is a poet, editor and writer of both fiction and non-fiction books, with many published volumes to his credit. He runs the Welsh Arts Council's Oriel Bookshop in Cardiff. You should read his book *How to Publish Your Poetry*, a mine of practical advice and information that will give you a valuable working knowledge of poetry publishing. Let's look at the points he makes:

Read other people's poetry
Writing good poetry is not just a matter of setting words out in lines, like chopped-up prose. Poetry editors despair at the lack of craftsmanship displayed by so many would-be poets. You need to

know how to combine the various elements of poetry to achieve the effects you want. The only way to do this is to study poetry closely, to analyse how its elements work – sound, rhyming patterns, rhythm, form, all have a part to play. You can learn how to study and analyse poetry from a book like *How Poetry Works* by Philip Davies Roberts.

Research the market
Read what is being published today. Unless you're in touch with current poetry publishing, you can't know what editors are looking for. Too many poets are sadly out of touch. Some even insist on sending verse of the 'Prithee, I come my troth to plight' vintage to contemporary poetry magazines. It isn't that editors only want 'modern' or experimental poetry. Far from it. Good contemporary poetry takes many forms. But editors still receive hopelessly archaic verse sent by poets who seem to have read nothing written this side of the Boer War.

Get to know the magazines you like, and support them
Every poetry magazine has its own distinctive flavour. When you find one whose poetry is in tune with your own preferences, concentrate on that magazine, at least to begin with. Don't even think about sending your poetry to a magazine you don't feel comfortable with, or in which you wouldn't be proud to be published. And don't send anything to a magazine you haven't seen – you don't know what kind of company you might be courting.

Subscribe to at least one magazine, more if you can afford it. It's in your own long-term interest to help keep the poetry scene alive. You need these magazines as much as they need you.

When you're ready to try for publication
Present your work as shown in the example on the facing page, typed, single-spaced with the stanzas clearly divided, and only one poem, however short, to a page.

Put your name and address on every sheet – on the back if you prefer. Anne Lewis-Smith, former editor of *Envoi*, says she published several poems that arrived without identification, and kept hoping that their authors would contact her to claim their entitlement of complimentary copies. They never did. *Envoi* is now edited by Roger Elkin – see page 181.

Unborn Children

These ghosts haunt differently, they come before,
Slowly, like secrets, pointing empty sleeves
From the margins of life, and promise more
Than the pattern anticipation weaves;
Some day I'll hear their laughter and their cries,
Touch their small hands and kiss their sleeping eyes.

They sing their coming in a swelling life,
The pleasure of our bodies' creating,
A helpless immortality my wife
And I can only tremble for, waiting
Until we hear their laughter and their cries
Touch their small hands and kiss their sleeping eyes.

They are my laughter at the frightened years
When pain was loneliness and solitude,
My freedom from my generation's tears,
A promise of a sure familiar mood
When I hear their laughter and their cries,
Touch their small hands and kiss their sleeping eyes.

Mike Pattinson

'Unborn Children' was published in *Acumen* magazine in October 1986, and is reproduced here in typescript form with Mike Pattinson's permission.

Never send anything (even an enquiry) without an SAE. And please don't ask for free copies 'to see if I like your magazine' or 'to study your requirements'. Small magazines struggle along on tiny budgets. Very few make even a marginal profit. You shouldn't expect them (or any other markets, for that matter) to subsidise your market study and your postage.

Saving money, time and aggravation
- Don't submit work to a major publishing house. A few, like Faber & Faber, do publish poetry, but say that they seldom find a beginner's work meets their standards. Wait till you have a respectable number of poems in print before you think about putting a collection together. And it's totally pointless to send single poems to big publishers.

- Don't send poetry to magazines that never publish it. They won't make an exception for you, however good you are.

- Don't send a saga the length of 'The Anglo-Saxon Chronicle' to a small magazine where it would fill a whole issue.

- Never send the same poem to more than one magazine at a time. This is known as 'multiple submission', and will do your reputation no good at all. You risk a double acceptance – not the triumph you might think. The editors concerned will be mutually embarrassed, and won't forgive you easily. Don't imagine they won't find out. Poetry editors see a lot of poetry magazines, and even if they don't see the gaffe for themselves, you can be sure some indignant poet will 'advise' them.

POETRY 'ON THE AIR'

Poet Alison Chisholm has recently succeeded Peggy Poole as Poetry Consultant to BBC Network Northwest's programme *Write Now*, a weekly half-hour of poems and stories from the region. Alison endorses the guidelines Peggy gave you in previous editions of this book, from her experience of selecting poems suitable for reading 'on the air'.

Outlets
If your local BBC or independent radio stations have no poetry programme, ask for one and organise area support. Poetry in the 90s has a much higher profile than it has had for many years. Studio managers should be persuaded of this and alerted to the chance of a successful programme which will involve local listeners.

Submissions
Submit as for a top-class magazine, with an SAE. Keep poems relatively short – a rough line limit of 40. (This does not mean the total exclusion of any longer work, particularly of a possible dramatic poem for several voices. In such a case it would be wise to write to the producer in advance explaining the content, and a decision will be made either to present an extra, one-off programme or to vary the style of the regular poetry programme for that one special occasion.)
    Do not use four-letter words, even if they are an integral part of a poem; this will jeopardise the programme.

Keep off politics, and ensure seasonal work arrives with plenty of time in hand. Humour is welcomed provided it is genuinely poetic and does not belong in a comedy programme. It's best to avoid nostalgic or pseudo-religious poems – huge amounts of these are received, but hardly ever used. Religious poems belong to religious programmes and, with a region of such variety, one person's nostalgia, unless of real quality, becomes someone else's boredom.

Reading
Many poets want to read their own work, but studios at the average broadcasting station are usually too heavily booked for this to be possible. It will depend on the producer and the length and format of the programme.

Payment
Do not expect this to be more than a token payment. Remember you are reaching a very wide audience.

A good poem should work as well on radio as in print, but it is important to remember that your audience is probably engaged in several other occupations while listening, so your poem needs to work instantly at one level while offering resonances of deeper meaning at the same time. For many years in producing BBC Radio Merseyside's poetry programme, I balanced on a tightrope, aiming both to attract the established poet without intimidating new poets from submitting their first attempts, and to present an enjoyable half-hour that might also succeed in converting a newcomer to poetry. Now, choosing poetry for *Write Now*, there is also the nature of the region to consider.

Peggy Poole

Study this market, too
Listen to as much broadcast poetry as you can. Details of poetry programmes are given every week in *Radio Times*. Local radio details are given for your region as a group. You will find these at the end of the TV programmes and at the start of the section for radio. *Write Now* is broadcast at different times and on different days on BBC Radio Merseyside, BBC Radio Lancashire, Greater Manchester Radio and BBC Radio Cumbria.

Do listen, even if your work is not being broadcast that week. Only by listening can you get the flavour of the programme.

Checklist for poetry submissions
1. Each poem is typed in the accepted form on a separate sheet of plain white A4 paper.

2. Your name and address appear on every sheet.

3. You've kept a note of where you're sending each poem, so that you don't risk a multiple submission, and kept a copy of each poem submitted.

4. You haven't sent more than six poems at any one time.

5. You've enclosed a stamped self-addressed envelope big enough and bearing adequate postage for the return of the whole batch.

Send your work to Alison Chisholm, 'Write Now', BBC North, 55 Paradise Street, Liverpool L1 3BP.

FINDING INFORMATION AND ADVICE

• **The Association of Little Presses (ALP)** issues *Poetry and Little Press Information (PALPI)*, and a current catalogue of *Little Press Books in Print*.

• **The Friends of the Arvon Foundation** produce a regular newsletter of information about competitions, festivals, writers' markets and literature.

• **The National Poetry Foundation** offers news of competitions and publications, and runs a poetry appraisal service for members.

• **The Oriel Bookshop** publishes *Small Press and Little Magazines of the UK and Ireland* (a regularly updated address list), a catalogue of recent poetry publications, a regular programme of literary events, a mail order 'books on books' service, and for writers living in Wales only, a criticism service subsidised by the Welsh Arts Council.

• **The Poetry Society** issues *Poetry Review Quarterly*, and also an information bulletin, advance notification of all Poetry Society events, access to special offers from the Poetry Society Bookshop, and a criticism service which anyone can use, although society members get reduced rates.

- **The Poetry Book Society** (a book club) offers a *Quarterly Bulletin*, a free annual poetry anthology, and discount prices on quality poetry books.

Books to help you
- Peter Finch, *How to Publish Your Poetry*. Probably the best investment you could make, full of information and sound practical advice.

- Alison Chisholm, *The Craft of Writing Poetry*. A much-published prize-winning poet takes you through the process of writing poetry, from the first spark of an idea to the final revision. Thoroughly practical, with detailed discussion and advice.

- Alison Chisholm, *A Practical Poetry Course*. A step-by-step guide to developing and sharpening poetic skills.

- Philip Davies Roberts, *How Poetry Works*. Explains the ways in which the various elements of English poetry – language, rhythm and metre, rhyming patterns and so on – contribute to a poetic work.

- Johnathon Clifford, *Metric Feet & Other Gang Members*. Self-published by one of the poetry world's more controversial figures. More valuable for its excellent analysis of poetic forms than its interesting but over-heated attack on the poetry establishment.

Magazines
Here are a few titles to introduce you to the wide range currently being published. As you become familiar with the poetry scene you'll discover many more – most magazines carry reviews of other publications both established and new.

- *Acumen*. Two issues a year. Publishes poetry, prose, reviews, interviews, articles on poets and poetry. 100-plus pages. Editor Patricia Oxley has no preferences on form or content, but you should avoid clichéd subjects.

- *Envoi*. Three issues a year. In 1991, after years of success with

Anne Lewis-Smith, the editor's mantle was donned by Roger Elkin. Roger has made extensive changes in editorial policy, including more comprehensive criticism of subscribers' work. Under his dedicated stewardship the magazine goes from strength to strength.

● *First Time.* Published twice a year. Dedicated to publishing new poetry by new poets. Editor Josephine Austin.

● *Outposts Poetry Quarterly.* Publishes a broad range of poetry by both new and established poets, also news and reviews. Now edited by Roland John, following more than 40 years under the care of its founder Howard Sergeant MBE.

● *Stand.* An international quarterly of new writing, publishing new poetry, fiction, plays, translations, criticism and art, and reviews of new poetry and fiction. Left of centre, and 'hospitable to a wide range of work. Free from prejudice, but socially conscious', the editors promise. They look for well made but exploratory writing. Carries lots of advertisements and information about literary publications. Editors Jon Silkin and Lorna Tracy.

● *Writers' Own Magazine.* Poetry and prose. Much of the content is by new or relatively new writers. Some news and reviews. A readers' letters section mainly providing mutual encouragement for its contributors. A useful and friendly starting point. Editor Eileen M Pickering.

● *Helicon* and *Reach.* Edited by Shelagh Nugent, these two poetry magazines are published by Cherrybite Publications. Shelagh also publishes short stories and articles in *Peninsular* and *Writers' Express.*

SONGWRITING

Do you dream of writing a 'standard', another 'White Christmas' or 'Stardust'? Do you watch the 'Song for Europe' contest and think 'I could write something better myself'? And maybe you could. From folk to rap, from traditional to hip-hop, there's always room for a good new song.

You can't write music?

You don't have to. What you need is a collaborator. You write the lyrics, your collaborator writes the music, and you take equal shares of any profits.

Look out for sharks

The 'shark' is the music business's equivalent of the vanity publisher. He asks for payment to write music to your lyrics. Don't fall for this. There hasn't yet been a successful song produced in this way. You'd be throwing your money away.

So how do you get started?

You can join a professional organisation, even if you're an absolute unpublished beginner. You'll have access to sound professional advice and guidance. If you need a collaborator, you'll be helped to find one who will work with you, on equal terms, with no money changing hands in either direction unless and until your song makes a profit.

The **Guild of International Songwriters & Composers** offers full membership to both amateur and professional songwriters. Services to members include:

- free advice and song assessment service
- how to promote songs to music publishers
- advice on recording, management and publishing contracts
- legal advisers
- publishing companies' names and addresses
- copyright of works
- who requires songs for publishing and recording
- collaboration service, songwriters' register
- song contests
- a free quarterly magazine, *Songwriting and Composing*.

Membership costs £35 in the UK and £45 outside the UK. If you would like a free copy of *Songwriting and Composing* magazine, send a stamped self-addressed A4 envelope, or phone or fax the Chairman, Roderick G Jones at the address given in Associations and Societies Open to Unpublished Writers (page 161).

And there are the books

- Stephen Citron, *Songwriting*. Takes you step by step through writing a song, illustrated with words and music from well-known songs. Full of ideas and tricks of the trade, it's particularly helpful for beginners. Covers lyrics, music, rhythm, form and style.

- Sheila Davis, *The Craft of Lyric Writing*. A guide to the art of writing words for and to music. Works through examples, and shows how to avoid common pitfalls.

- *Songwriter's Market*. An annual guide to markets for songs. Like all the Writers' Digest Books market guides, it includes advice on writing and tips to help you get your work published.

GREETING CARDS

This is where you scout around the shops again, but now you're interested in displays of greeting cards. Greeting cards are very big business. According to recent figures from America, their citizens send out over 10,000,000 'conventional' greeting cards every day of the year. And 'conventional' cards are only one category of the six basic types of card. The others are 'informal', 'juvenile', 'humorous', 'studio' and 'inspirational'.

There's an expanding market here in the UK, too, and many card companies buy ideas from freelance writers.

Take time to study the cards. Could you write the kind of copy they use? Many companies print their address on the back of their cards. Contact them to ask if they issue guidelines for copywriters or, if they don't, whether they have any preferences with regard to presentation. Some companies are very specific about this, others don't mind so long as the ideas are laid out clearly. If there are no instructions, type one idea per sheet on A5 paper, with your name and address on every sheet. (Hanson White Ltd have recently asked their copywriters to type as many ideas as clarity allows on an A4 sheet, to help conserve paper.)

They might not buy anything from your first batch, but if a company likes the kind of work you send them they'll add your name to their list of copywriters and will send you regular details of their current requirements and urgent 'wants'. Deadlines for seasonal submissions vary from company to company.

At present, your best chance of selling is in the humorous lines. Study each company's cards closely. While at first glance many of the lines appear similar, analysis will show that every company has its own style.

Here's an idea that Hanson White bought from the author, reproduced here with the company's permission. (You'll almost invariably be required to sell all rights to your greeting card copy – very few companies pay on a royalty basis.)

Mother's Day:
Page 1: You're a Mum in a million. Thanks for putting up with all the naughty things I've done.
Page 3: ...Good job you don't know about the rest!
     Happy Mother's Day

The card made from this idea, illustrated by a commissioned artist, won the 'Mother's Day Best Humorous/Cute Card' category in the 1991 Greetings Industry Spring Awards. It's a good example of a 'sendable' card which would appeal to a wide range of buyers. The judges said they 'could all relate to it'.

Rates of payment vary, but most companies pay from £25 upwards for each idea bought (some pay much more). You'll find information about American greeting card markets in the American *Writer's Market* which you can buy through bookstores like Waterstone's.

For UK markets, your best source of information, besides the cards themselves, is the monthly *Greetings*, the magazine of the Greeting Card and Calendar Association – see Information Services and Sources (Page 166). You'll find some addresses of UK companies under Greeting Card Companies on page 173.

A book to inspire you
From the ever dependable Writer's Digest Books comes *How to Write and Sell Greeting Cards, Bumper Stickers, T-shirts and Other Fun Stuff* – a mouthful of a title, but a treasury of tips and examples from a former Hallmark staff writer.

12
Writing for Radio, Screen and Stage

RADIO AND TELEVISION

The **British Broadcasting Corporation** (BBC) is one of the biggest potential markets for freelance writers. Radios Three and Four broadcast around 500 plays a year between them, and around 50 of these are written by new writers. Since the axing in 1991 of the radio and television script units, there is now no specific way of getting your material looked at, so your best plan is to study the work of producers whose style and choice of material appeals to you, and send your script (with an SAE) to the producer c/o the programme, at the address of the radio station or TV channel.

Short stories for radio
Scheduling changes at BBC Radio Four have resulted in the best-known short story outlet, *Morning Story*, being dropped. However, there is now an afternoon *Storytime* slot, for which short stories are needed. The flavour of stories used latterly in *Morning Story* was distinctly different from the generally rather bland tales that made up most of its previous content. This change continued with *Storytime*, where the stories that are wanted now deal with current issues, contemporary themes and topical concerns, reflecting the times and conditions in which we live. The required length is as before, around 2,300 words.

The producer's name is given after each broadcast, and it could pay to target a producer whose choices seem compatible with the kind of stories you write. Rosemary Horstmann's book *Writing for Radio* is helpful on writing for speech.

Radio drama
The **BBC's Radio Drama Department** broadcasts plays, adaptations, series and serials. You can get a free leaflet, *Writing Plays for Radio* from the Chief Producer, Plays (Radio Drama) at Broadcasting House.

Light Entertainment Radio

Light Entertainment Radio is interested in receiving scripts or ideas for half-hour sit-coms or panel games. There are writers' guidelines available from The Senior Producer Scripts (Light Entertainment Radio), BBC, Langham Street, London W1A 1AA (enclose an A4 SAE).

Topical programmes like *Week Ending* and *The News Huddlines* use a lot of freelance material. Both these programmes hold weekly meetings for uncommissioned writers during their run, and any writer is welcome to attend. The meetings are held at Broadcasting House in Room 1022 (The Writers' Room): 1pm Tuesdays for *The News Huddlines*, and 1pm Wednesdays for *Week Ending*.

Local radio

There could be openings for all kinds of material on your local radio stations, both BBC and independent. The only way to find out what kind of material might be suitable is to listen in. If you think you can offer something interesting and suitable, contact the station manager. Both the *Writers' & Artists' Yearbook* and *The Writer's Handbook* carry comprehensive lists of addresses, the latter giving detailed information about personnel.

Television drama

BBC TV is interested in original 60-minute plays and 90-minute screenplays dealing with contemporary themes. The fewer the locations and the smaller the casts needed, the greater your advantage. This is a difficult market to penetrate, and if you've no track record and nobody knows your name your script might be returned unread. Best to make your mark on radio first – see Wally K Daly's remarks on page 144.

Television light entertainment

All submissions for sketch shows like *Smith & Jones*, *Naked Video*, *Hale & Pace* and so on are considered – you don't need a track record to succeed here if you can supply the right kind of material. You need to study the shows very closely – a video recorder is essential – and you need to send your material at the appropriate time. Call the BBC (ask for the **Comedy Script Unit**) for schedules of upcoming series.

The **Comedy Department** is always interested in new 30-minute series, studio-based in the main for preference to keep costs down. They want to see original formats rather than rehashing of existing programmes.

Starting out

If you have no track record don't start by writing for TV drama, except for fun – you'd have more chance of winning the pools than having your play bought and transmitted. The best market for new playwrights is without a doubt BBC Radio. The best slot length is half-hour, followed by *Afternoon Theatre* (45 or 55 minutes).

If you are an intellectual giant write half-hour plays for Radio 3, they are always desperate for a good product.

If you have a sense of humour let it show in your scripts. 'Funny' is more saleable than 'Doom and Gloom'.

Don't waste time entering competitions – back to winning the pools again – simply send your first script, typed, double spaced, A4 paper, good sized left margin, off to BBC Script Unit*, BBC, Broadcasting House, London W1A 1AA, then get on with writing the next. No point in waiting to see how they like the first – it's going to be three months before you hear about that one, unless it's an absolute 'no-no' when it will be back in two.

The only book on the subject I would advise buying is *Writing for the BBC*, a BBC publication that gives all available markets, plus demonstration layout.

See – easy, isn't it?

Wally K Daly, former Chair, Writers' Guild of Great Britain, writer of drama and television comedy for both radio and TV; also of five stage plays and three musicals, the best known being Follow the Star (music, Jim Parker).

*Note: The BBC Script Unit no longer exists – see page 142.

Is the money good?

Yes, it can be very good, especially if you can establish yourself as a valued regular contributor. What you'll be paid depends on how well established you are. You can check current rates of pay with the BBC.

The Comedy Writers Association

The Comedy Writers Association UK was formed in the early 1980s to promote good comedy writing and to encourage and advise new writers. Members sell to radio and TV outlets worldwide. They're helped by the lively exchange of experience, techniques and market information.

Writing saleable comedy material is a specialised discipline. You have to know what's wanted where and at the right time. Every comedian has his own style. Study that style and tailor your work to suit. For example, a joke written for Ken Dodd would be no good for Roy Walker. In situation comedy, keep characters and sets to a minimum. Avoid too much outside filming. Study TV programmes and comedians. And accept rejections – they're part of every comedy writer's life.

Ken Rock, President, Comedy Writers Association UK

If you'd like to know more about the Comedy Writers Association UK, contact Ken Rock at the CWAUK address given in the appendices.

Don't leave it all to the men

Why do most women assume that only men can write funny material? You'll probably find it quite hard to think of more than a handful of women who have made their mark in comedy writing. Victoria Wood, of course, Carla Lane, French and Saunders...but not many more.

For centuries women have laughed at jokes told and written by men. Yet despite being successful as writers, few women attempt to write comedy. Being a keen observer of human nature, seeing the funny side of life, and the ability to study comedy writing techniques are not exclusive to men.

Joyce Lister

Joyce Lister has built a successful second career as a comedy writer, after illness forced her to give up her nursing activities. She has sold material to, among others, *The Grumbleweeds* (Granada TV), *Fast Forward* (BBC2 for children), *Little and Large* and Radio Luxembourg. She achieved her first success with a series of humorous articles based on her nursing experience, published in her local paper. She's also a talented and successful writer of greeting card material. Have you got Joyce's kind of talent? She would like to see many more women writing in the comedy field.

A specialist service

Rosemary Horstmann, author of *Writing for Radio*, brings her expertise and long experience as a producer, broadcaster, scriptwriter, journalist, tutor and administrator to a service designed to give constructive advice and supportive encouragement to authors who want to write for broadcasting.

Rosemary offers script evaluation, coaching in interviewing techniques, and tuition in the use of a professional tape recorder and the editing of tape. Tuition sessions on scriptwriting and her other services can be arranged either one-to-one or on a group basis. Contact Rosemary for details of services and current charges.

Recommended reading

• Rosemary Horstmann, *Writing for Radio*. Practical advice from a highly experienced producer, writer, tutor and lecturer.

• William Smethurst, *How to Write for Television*. The complete guide to breaking into this lucrative market.

• Ronald Tobias, *The Insider's Guide to Writing for Screen and Television*.

• *The Stage and Television Today*.

WRITING FOR FILM AND VIDEO

Most film and video companies will only look at material submitted through an established agent. You could try contacting one of the agents listed in the *Writers' & Artists' Yearbook* and *The Writer's Handbook*. Make sure you approach only those who specify an interest in this field. Your chances are slim, however, unless you can present some reasonably impressive work-in-progress and preferably also a portfolio of published work. They're not really likely to be interested in a total beginner.

As a newcomer, your best first move is to send for details of the **London Screenwriters Workshop**. Although this association is based in London, it caters for many out-of-town and overseas members, too. And you don't need any track record to join.

WRITING FOR THE STAGE

Your best starting point as a new playwright is a local repertory theatre or amateur dramatic group. If you have no track record at all, it's unrealistic to expect to see your name in lights in London's West End with your first effort. Not impossible, but not likely.

However, management companies send scouts to repertory productions all over the country. They're always on the lookout for original and potentially profitable plays and yours might be 'spotted'.

It's usually best to write first and ask if the company would like to see your script. Give all the relevant details: type of play, how many sets, how many characters and so on.

Never send anyone your only copy.

Read up on contracts before you sign any agreement. *The Writers' & Artists' Yearbook* explains contracts in detail.

Playwrights' groups

Ask your nearest **Regional Arts Office** (you'll find the phone number in your local directory, or look it up in the *Writers' & Artists' Yearbook*) for details of playwrights' associations in your area. Most of these groups hold readings and can arrange for script criticism.

The **Player-Playwrights** society reads, performs and discusses plays and scripts, to help members improve and market their work.

Membership of the **New Playwrights' Trust (NPT)** is open to all playwrights, aspiring playwrights, and those interested in developing and encouraging new playwriting. There are workshops, a script-reading service, a writer/company Link Service and a monthly newsletter.

Getting your play published

It's well worth trying to get your play published, especially if it's been considered good enough to be given live performance by a local company. You can send your script to **Samuel French Ltd**, who publish nothing else but plays. If French's publish it, they'll include it in their *Guide to Selecting Plays*, a substantial catalogue of plays intended for performance by amateur dramatic groups.

You don't need an agent to approach French's, but they prefer that the play should have been tried out in some kind of performance, because performance reveals flaws that might have been overlooked in the written work, and which you could correct before submitting the piece for professional consideration. They make no assessment charge. French's will send you, on request and free of charge, their mail order list of books and cassettes on all the media and performing arts: writing, acting, production, make-up and so on, from Shakespeare to pantomime. (It helps if you can specify your area or areas of interest.)

ACT ONE SCENE 4

(Into Daniel's fantasy) The stage remains in total darkness for a few seconds. Then we hear a voice off. It is Daniel's own voice but distorted and amplified to sound God-like.

VOICE: In the beginning there was the stadium. But the stadium was empty and the ground without shape or form.

There is a roll of thunder and a flash of lightning lights up the stage for a second. We see a deserted football stadium.

Darkness was everywhere. Then the spirit of God moved in the wilderness and said: Let there be light.

Lights up. But they are floodlights as at a football stadium.

This was the first day and it was good. But God saw that the stadium was empty and the gates were poor so he didst command: Upon these terraces let there come forth all creatures great and small.

Football fans enter. Bewildered at first. Newly born.

And he called these creatures (*pause*) fans.

Explosion of music. Cheering etc. It stops as suddenly as it began.

Then God blessed these creatures and said unto them: Go forth and multiply.

FAN: He said what?

VOICE: You heard. Go forth and multiply.

FAN: Right lads. Let's get at it. (*They try*)

VOICE: And this was the second day and it was good. (*Pause*) But not that good for he had not yet invented women. (*Groans from fans*)

FANS: (Chant) Why are we waiting? Why are we waiting...?

Fig. 14. Example of how to set out a play script.

Theatre production companies

You could try making contact with some of the professional production companies who actively seek new writers' work. You'll find an encouragingly long list of companies in *The Writer's Handbook*. Choose those who specify an interest in new writing.

Specific requirements

Production companies, like book and magazine publishers, have their own individual styles and requirements. Very few plays would suit them all. Find out as much as you can about a company's preferences before you approach them. This groundwork could pay good dividends. Study the entries in *The Writer's Handbook*, and read *The Stage and Television Today*. These will give you a good idea of what production companies are currently interested in.

Read the small ads in *The Stage and Television Today*, where you'll often find small companies asking for scripts.

When you send a script to a production company, use the standard layout. Make it absolutely clear who is saying what, and which lines are speech and which are stage directions. Study the sample script in Figure 14, an extract from Steve Wetton's play *King of the Blues*.

Steve also offers you this tip: Nowadays, directors and actors tend to fall about laughing when they see the kind of detailed stage directions that used to litter playscripts. Directions like 'Jeremy moves downstage right, knocks his pipe out in the ashtray to the left of the paperweight and then goes to lean nonchalantly with his right elbow on the shelf above the mantelpiece' are a total giveaway of a writer's inexperience.

Grants and bursaries

The Arts Council of Great Britain gives details of various forms of financial assistance in its brochure *Theatre Writing Schemes*. For a copy of the brochure, and any other information you need, contact the Drama Director, The Arts Council of Great Britain.

Some companies to approach

Here are the detailed requirements of three companies who welcome new playscripts:

Paines Plough, New Writing New Theatre

Takes new plays on tour nationally. A Readers' Panel reports on all scripts submitted (this can take two or three months). Send two

SAEs, for response and return of script. They offer the following tips about submitting scripts:

- *Do* take care with the layout. It's especially important to distinguish between dialogue and stage directions. Underline all stage directions or type them in capitals.

- *Do* put the full name of the character (not an initial or other abbreviation) in capitals on the left hand side of the page before every speech. Spread out generously. Never use both sides of the paper.

- *Do* enclose a suitably sized SAE.

- *Do* include a brief synopsis, fewer than 200 words.

- *Do* make the cover of the play look interesting in some way.

- *Don't* send more than one play at a time. The envelopes that collect most dust are the ones containing 'a selection' of the author's work. Find out about the company you're writing to and send them the play you think most appropriate – if they want more, they'll ask for more.

- *Don't* say too much in your covering letter. Avoid a detailed explanation of your play's themes and meaning – if these are not clear in the play itself, then you've written it badly.

- *Don't* waste a fortune on postage. Send out a synopsis with a sample scene, and find out which companies are really interested.

- *Don't* pester people. Wait at least three months before enquiring about a response.

The Traverse Theatre, Edinburgh
One of the country's foremost producers of work by new writers. They read everything that comes in, but say it helps if authors observe a few basic requirements.

- *Do* limit the cast to not more than nine characters. Include a character list and the number of actors required.

- *Do* include a word or two about the setting ('London in the Blitz', 'contemporary living room' and so on).

- *Do* remember that small underfunded theatres like the Traverse can't do spectacular effects with swimming pools, live animals and the like.

- *Do* note that the company looks for plays that say something new. There would be little interest in scripts about mid-life crises set in kitchen and living room, for example.

- *Do* please use some kind of binding. Readers take piles of scripts home to read – and loose scripts don't mix with children and pets.

Any play you submit to the Traverse Theatre should not have been performed professionally before. Send the full script, not a synopsis.

You'll receive a reader's report from a panel of directors, actors, writers and academics. This can take up to three months, so be patient. Perhaps one author in 20 will be asked to see them. One in 500 might get a workshop reading, and one in 1,000 a full production. If your play is thought to be good but not suitable for the Traverse, they'll advise you about other possible outlets.

Liverpool Playhouse
The Liverpool Playhouse has an active policy of promoting new work. They look for exciting, innovative work from new play-wrights, 'the voice of the 90s', with a real feeling of truth in the writing. The company is particularly supportive to local writers through workshops and writer surgeries. The following are a few guidelines:

- All new scripts are welcome. They are read by a pool of readers who then submit reports to the Artistic Director.

- Scripts can be sent straight to the theatre. Everything should be very clearly addressed.

- Scripts should be typed, with all pages numbered.

- There are no stipulated criteria in terms of content, cast size and so on, but huge casts are difficult.

Recommended reading

- Richard Andrews, *Writing a Musical*. The first practical guide to cover the whole topic from the basic concept to the first night. Detailed and easy-to-read guidance from an experienced professional who is actively involved in West End theatre. (See Façade, below.)

- Dilys Gater, *How to Write a Play for the Amateur Stage*.

- Steve Gooch, *Writing a Play*.

French's Theatre Bookshop will send you a list of current books relevant to writing for the theatre.

An introductory course and workshops for writing for musical theatre

Façade was founded in 1988 by Richard Andrews and Mary Stewart-David to create, promote and produce new works in musical theatre.

The **Façade** Partnership offers services ranging from an information base through casting to budgeting and general management.

Since 1989, Façade has been running an introductory course called 'Making a Musical', on which Richard Andrews' new book *Writing a Musical* is based.

Other activities to help and encourage new writers and composers include Readers' Reports and organising workshops and showcases.

If you're interested in writing for the musical theatre and would like to know more about Façade, Richard will be happy to hear from you. The address is under 'Services'.

Glossary

Advance. A sum paid to an author in advance of publication of his book. The usual terms are that the publisher will retain the author's royalty until the advance is paid off, after which the author receives his agreed share of the profits.

Agreement. See Contract.

Anthology. A collection of stories, poems and so on, which may or may not have been published before.

Article. A piece of prose writing that deals with a single subject (less commonly with several related subjects).

Autobiography. A person's life story, written by himself.

Balloon. A balloon- or bubble-shaped outline containing text.

Bi-monthly. Every two months.

Biography. A person's life as investigated and evaluated by someone else.

Blurb. Promotional text on the flap of a book jacket or the outside back cover of a paperback, sometimes exaggerating its worth.

Bullet. A large dot preceding and adding emphasis to an item in a book or article. Also called a stab point.

Byline. A line at the head or foot of a piece of writing identifying the writer: 'by Adam Ampersand'.

©. A symbol signifying that a work is protected by copyright.

'Category' fiction. Fiction written to fit into a specific genre: romance, Western, thriller and so on.

Collaboration. The working together of two or more people to produce a work, sometimes published under a single pseudonym. (For example, 'Ellery Queen' who is/are Frederic Dannay and Manfred B Lee.)

Contract. A signed document, an agreement between publisher and author specifying in exact detail the responsibilities each party undertakes in the writing, production and marketing of a book, in terms of payment, assignation of rights and so on.

Copy. Matter to be typeset. Usually refers to the prepared typescript.

Copyright. The exclusive right in his own work of an author or other designated party, as defined by law.

Copywriting. Writing material for use in advertisements, publicity material and the like.

Critique. A critical examination and written report on a work.

Deadline. The latest date or time by which a job must be finished.

Draft. A preliminary version.

Edition. One printing of a book. A second or subsequent edition will have alterations, sometimes substantial, compared with the previous edition.

Editorial policy. The editor's overall concept of the kind of publication he wants to produce.

FBSR (First British Serial Rights). The right to publish a story or article for the first time and once only in the UK. Not applicable to books.

Feature. A magazine or newspaper piece, an article which is not one of a series.

Fiction. Writing that is not and does not pretend to be truth, but which is entirely drawn from the imagination.

Flyer. A leaflet sent out in the post.

Folio. 1. A leaf, that is, two pages of a book. 2. A page number. 3. A manuscript page. 4. A postal workshop system.

'Freebie'. A slang term for a freesheet, a publication distributed free to householders, travellers *etc*. Anything given without charge.

Freelance. A self-employed person who sells his or her services or written work to a publisher for an agreed fee. A writer/journalist who sells work to various publications but is not employed by any one publisher. (Derives from the mercenary knights and soldiers who wandered Europe after the Crusades, hiring out their services, complete with lances, wherever they could.)

Genre. A literary species or specific category, for example Westerns, detective stories *etc*.

Ghosting/ghost writing. Writing a book in conjunction with someone else (usually a celebrity but could be anyone with a saleable story) as if it had been written by that other person, with no credit given to the writer.

GSM. Grammes per square metre (grammage), the specification of paper weights.

Hack. A derogatory term applied to a person who writes primarily for money.

HB. Abbreviation for 'hardback', a book with a stiff board cover.

Imprint. 1. The name of the printer with the place and time of printing, required by law in many countries for papers, books and so on meant for publication. 2. The name of the publisher with place and date of publication.

Internet. A global collection of computer networks with a common addressing scheme.

IRC. International Reply Coupon, a voucher sold at post offices worldwide, equivalent to the value of the minimum postal rate for a letter posted in the country from which the reply will come.

ISBN. International Standard Book Number, a unique ten-digit reference number given to every book published, to identify its area of origin, publisher, title and check control.

ISSN. International Standard Series Number, an eight-digit reference number given to periodical publications, used in a scheme similar to the ISBN system.

Journalist. A person who writes for a journal, newspaper, periodical, and so on, as distinct from authoring books.

Layout. The overall appearance of a script or a printed page.

Libel. A printed or broadcast malicious and defamatory statement.

Literary agent. A person who acts on behalf of an author in his dealings with publishers, offering his work and negotiating the contract for work the agent places. Agents always work on commission, usually 10–15 per cent. They don't make any money from your work till you do.

Mainstream fiction. A term applied to literary subjects that are traditional or current, as distinct from category or genre fiction.

Market study. The analytical study of the author's possible points of sale.

Matter. Manuscript or other copy which is to be printed, or type that is composed for printing.

Media. Sources of information, such as newspapers, magazines, radio, TV and so on. (Plural of medium, that is, 'medium of communication'.)

Multiple submissions. The sending of the same ms to more than one editor at a time. In general, this is not an acceptable practice.

Novel. A fictional story written in prose, of any length but not usually less than 50,000 words.

'On spec'/on speculation. Usually applied to writing submitted to an editor on a purely speculative basis, that is, not by invitation or commission. Also applied to work sent at an editor's invitation but without any commitment from him to accept the piece.

Outline. A sketched-out structure of a piece, showing what it will contain and in what order, but without detail. See also Synopsis.

Out of print. No longer on the publisher's list. That is, no longer available except from libraries or second-hand book dealers.

'Over the transom'. American slang for the arrival of unsolicited mss.

PB. Abbreviation for 'paperback', a book whose covers are made of paper, card or laminated card.

Photo-journalism. Journalism in which the text is of secondary importance to the photographs.

Photo-story script. A story told in the form of a sequence of photographs with captions.

Picture-agency. An organisation which keeps photographs and/or illustrations in store and leases reproduction rights to writers and publishers.

Picture fees. 1. Fees paid by an author or publisher for the right to reproduce illustrations in which he does not hold the copyright. 2. Fees paid by a publisher to an author or journalist for the right to reproduce his illustrations.

Picture-story script. A story told in a sequence of artist-drawn pictures, with dialogue shown in balloons, and perhaps with supplementary captions.

Plagiarism. The use without permission, whether deliberate or accidental, of work in which the copyright is held by someone else.

Plot. The storyline, the central thread of a story with which everything else that happens is interwoven.

PLR (Public Lending Right). A system of monetary reward for authors, based on the number of times their works are borrowed from public libraries. The award any one writer will receive depends on the book meeting certain conditions and being borrowed a minimum number of times.

Professional journal. A publication produced specifically for circulation in a particular profession, for example *The Lancet* (medicine).

Proofs. An impression or series of impressions of the typeset matter for checking and correction before the final printing.

Proposal. A suggested idea for a book, usually put to the publisher in the form of an initial query ('Would you be interested in . . .?'), then as a synopsis of the whole work, with a sample chapter or two.

Publisher's reader. A person employed by a publisher to evaluate a manuscript and to submit a written summary and report, to help the publisher assess its potential as a published work.

Readership. A collective term applied to the people who habitually read a particular publication.

Reading fee. A fee charged by an agent, magazine or publisher to read a submitted ms. Usually refundable in the event of acceptance and publication.

Rights. Those parts of an author's copyright which he leases to a publisher as specified in a contract.

Royalty. A percentage of the selling price of a book payable to the author under the terms of his contract. How much he receives depends on the percentage agreed and on the number of copies sold.

SAE (US SASE). Stamped addressed envelope (US self-addressed stamped envelope). An envelope addressed back to the sender, and bearing adequate postage stamps.

'Scissors-and-paste job'. A contemptuous term applied to work that consists of material 'lifted' from reference books, encyclopedias, magazines, and so on, rearranged and then passed off as an original piece of writing.

Screenplay. A film script that includes cinematic information – for example, camera movements – as well as dialogue.

'Slush-pile'. A term applied to the unsolicited mss which accumulate in an editorial office. So-called because of the sentimental and emotional content of a large proportion of these mss.

Small presses. Small businesses, often one-person operations, producing publications ranging from duplicated pamphlets to bound books, and of highly variable production quality. Seldom profitable, and usually financed by their proprietors and/or other enthusiasts.

Staff-writer (US staffer). A writer employed and salaried by a publisher, as distinct from a freelance.

Storyline. The sequence of events that keeps the action of a plot moving forward: 'And then... and then... and next...'

Strap/strapline. An identification line at the top of a manuscript page.

Submission. A manuscript that is sent – submitted – to a publisher, with a view to possible publication.

Subsidiary rights. A term usually applied to rights other than UK book publication rights. For example, film and TV rights, foreign language rights, serial rights and so on.

Synopsis. A précis or condensed version of the theme and contents of a book, giving a clear outline and breakdown of the proposed text.

Syntax. The way in which words or phrases are put together.

Taboos. Subjects, words, references that are not acceptable to certain publications.

Technical writing. The writing of company and product manuals, reports, engineering and computing manuals and so on.

Text. The body of typeset matter in a book, as distinct from headings, footnotes, illustrations, and such like.

Textbooks. Usually applied to books written for the educational market.

Theme. The subject of a story, the thread that links the narrative. For example, a moral concept – 'crime doesn't pay', 'love conquers all' – or a specific human quality, like courage or greed, self-sacrifice or failure. Not to be confused with the plot.

Trade journal. A publication produced for circulation among practitioners and companies in a particular trade or industry, for example *The Bookseller, The Grocer*.

Unsolicited manuscript/unsolicited submission. A piece of work sent to a publisher entirely without invitation.

Usual terms/usual rates. The usual rate of payment which a publication offers to freelance writers.

'Vanity publishing'. A term applied to the publication of work on behalf of an author who pays someone else to publish the work for him.

Voucher copy. A copy of a single issue of a publication, sent free to a writer whose work appears in that issue, as a courtesy and as evidence (to vouch) that the work has in fact been published.

Word processor (WP). A machine which uses computer logic to accept, store and retrieve material for editing and eventual printing out in typewritten or printed form.

Workshop. A group of people meeting to exchange opinions and constructive suggestions on current work, usually under the guidance of a writer/tutor.

World Wide Web (also referred to as WWW and The Web). A network of graphic and text document 'pages' linked together on the Internet.

Writers' circle. A group of people meeting to read, discuss and possibly criticise each other's work. Differs from a workshop in that the work is usually done at home before instead of during the meeting.

Writers' seminar. A meeting of writers, usually lasting at least one day, where there are guest speakers, discussions, possibly workshops, and where writers can make contact with other writers, both published and unpublished.

Yearbook. A book published annually, reviewing the past year's events and/or updating information.

Associations and Societies Open to Unpublished Writers

Association of Little Presses (ALP). New members always welcome. Formed to bring together, inform and assist small presses (usually one- or two-person outfits) publishing poetry, short stories and other literature. Issues a (roughly) bi-monthly newsletter of information about the world of small presses, with printing and production tips, sources of stationery supplies, services and so on, *Poetry and Little Press Information (PALPI)* magazine, and the current catalogue of *Little Press Books in Print*. For subscription details, contact Stan Trevor, 86 Lytton Road, Oxford OX4 3NZ. Tel: (01865) 718266.

British Amateur Press Association. Brings together people interested in the various arts and crafts of journalism as a hobby. Details from British Amateur Press Association, Michaelmas, Cimarron Close, South Woodham Ferrers, Essex CM3 5PB.

British Fantasy Society. Covers the fantasy, horror and science fiction fields. Publishes a regular newsletter of information and reviews of books, films and events, plus its own magazine *Dark Horizons*, containing fiction and articles. Organises an annual fantasy conference, 'Fantasycon', and the British Fantasy Awards. Benefits include contact with like-minded writers and fans. Membership open to all. Subscription and membership details from The Secretary, BFS, 2 Harwood Street, Stockport, Cheshire SK4 1JJ.

British Science Fiction Association. Covers science fiction and related genres, and is intended for authors, publishers and fans. Members receive three magazines per annum covering news and information, amateur fiction and critical studies. An important element of the association is the Orbiter group, which offers support, constructive criticism, and allows members to study each others' fiction. Details of subscription and membership from Alison Cook, 52 Wood Hill Drive, Grove, Wantage, Oxfordshire OX12 0DF.

Bureau of Freelance Photographers (BFP). Membership open to professional and amateur photographers and writers. Offers a monthly newsletter full of factual, verified information on current markets for photographs and photojournalism, an advisory service, a fee recovery service, and discounts on photographic goods and services. Publishes an annual *BFP Freelance Photographers' Market Handbook*. The annual fee covers all the above. For more details (including a free two-month introductory offer) contact John Tracy, Bureau of Freelance Photographers, Focus House, 497 Green Lanes, London N13 4BP. Tel: (0181) 882 3315.

Comedy Writers Association UK. A non-profit-making club to help new and established comedy writers sell their work. Aims to help and encourage fellow writers, to provide members with regular market information, and to promote comedy writing. There's a monthly newsletter, market information bulletins, and meetings in various parts of the country (members are encouraged to contact each other), visits to radio and TV studios, rehearsals and programme recordings, a library geared to comedy writing, and an annual weekend conference. CWA members work at professional levels, and if you haven't already sold material to radio and/or TV you'll be asked to complete a set of test exercises which will be assessed by the committee. Details of subscription and membership from the President, Ken Rock, 61 Parry Road, Ashmore Park, Wolverhampton, West Midlands WV11 2PS. Tel: (01902) 722729.

Fellowship of Christian Writers. Membership open to 'those who desire to serve Jesus Christ in the realm of writing'. For those interested in all types of writing: novels, children's books, articles, poetry, radio... There's a manuscript criticism service, fees by arrangement. Has a country-wide network of writers' groups. For details of subscription and membership send an SAE to Hon Secretary Janet Hall, Shee-Dy-Vea, 151A Bedford Road, Marston Morteyne, Bedfordshire MK43 0LD. Tel: (01234) 767470.

The Friends of Arvon Foundation. Active in support of the Arvon Foundation. Issues a regular newsletter of information about events, competitions, writers' markets and literature, plus details of current and projected Arvon writers' courses. For subscription and membership details send an SAE to Joan Thornton, 6 Church Street, Darfield, Yorkshire S73 9LG.

The Ghost Story Society. For anyone interested in supernatural fiction, especially traditional ghost stories. Members receive three magazines per annum, with details of new books, films and television shows. Publishes letters and new fiction. Subscription and membership details from The Ghost Story Society, Ashcroft, 2 Abbottsford Drive, Penyffordd, Chester CH4 0JG.

Guild of International Songwriters and Composers (GISC). Aims to give advice and guidance to its songwriter, composer and home recordist members. Open to amateur as well as professional songwriters. Offers members song assessments, collaboration between lyric writers and composers, information on music publishers' requirements, advice about copyright, contracts, demonstration tapes, presentation and so on. A free quarterly magazine, *Songwriting and Composing*, is issued to members. Annual subscription £35 UK (£45 outside the UK). For a free copy of the magazine and details of membership, send a large stamped self-addressed envelope to the chairman, Roderick G Jones, The Guild of International Songwriters and Composers, Sovereign House, 12 Trewartha Road, Praa Sands, Penzance, Cornwall TR20 9ST. Tel: (01736) 762826. Fax: (01736) 763328. E-mail: Songmag@aol.com and Internet web site: http://www/icn.co.uk/gisc.html

The Historical Novel Society. Aims to promote all aspects of historical fiction. Issues a magazine, *Solander*, twice a year, carrying articles by prominent historical novelists (Bernard Cornwell, E V Thompson, Helen Carey...), reviews of the best historical fiction, information about events, clubs and societies. Organises local events in partnership with Dillons, and runs national short story competitions for first-time authors. For details of membership and subscription send an SAE to Richard Lee, Secretary, The Historical Novel Society, Marine Cottage, The Strand, Starcross, Devon EX6 8NY.

London Screenwriters Workshop. Open to anyone interested in writing for film and TV, and to those working in these and related media. Practical workshops are held in London, and out-of-town members can send in scripts for reading and criticism by practising screenwriters. Issues a newsletter, and advises members about agents and producers. Has members throughout the UK and beyond. For details of subscription and membership, contact Paul Gallacher or Anji Loman Field, London Screenwriters Workshop, 84 Wardour Street, London W1V 3LF. Tel: (0171) 434 0942.

National Poetry Foundation. Offers a bi-annual magazine, *Pause*, appraisal of members' poems, possible publication in *Pause*, possible eventual publication of a book of your poems (at no cost to you), news of competitions and literature, all covered by the annual membership fee of £20. The generous sponsorship of Rosemary Arthur now enables the Foundation to make grants to other poetry magazines. For full details contact the Founder, Johnathon Clifford, 27 Mill Road, Fareham, Hampshire PO16 0TH. Tel: (01329) 822218.

New Playwrights Trust. Open to all playwrights and others interested in the development of playwriting. Offers comprehensive information services, workshops and a writer/company Link Service. For subscription details, contact New Playwrights Trust, Interchange Studios, 15 Dalby Street, London NW5 3NQ. Tel: (0171) 284 2818.

The Penman Club. World-wide membership open to all writers. Membership includes free criticism of mss, general and marketing advice, and a free library service (you pay only the postage). For details of subscription and membership fees, contact the General Secretary, Mark Sorrell, 185 Daws Heath Road, Benfleet, Essex SS7 2TF.

Player-Playwrights (at St Augustine's Church Hall, Queens Gate, London SW1). President Jack Rosenthal. A long-established society of amateur and professional writers and actors. Welcomes newcomers to play and television writing. Members' scripts are performed, then discussed. Contact the Secretary, Peter Thompson, 9 Hillfield Park, London N10 3QT. Tel: (0181) 883 0371.

The Poetry Book Society. A book club. Subscription covers a quarterly bulletin, a free annual poetry anthology, and the opportunity to buy quality poetry books at discount prices. For details of current subscription rates, contact the Administrator, Betty Redpath, Freepost, Book House, 45 East Hill, London SW18 2BR.

The Poetry Society. Membership open to all. Membership fee covers a quarterly magazine of new verse, views and criticism, *Poetry Review*, a quarterly newsletter, *Poetry News*, promotions and events, competitions and awards, a manuscript diagnosis service (reduced rates for members), a library service, a Poetry Café and much more. For full details of membership fees and services, contact The Poetry Society, 22 Betterton Street, London WC2H 9BU. Tel: (0171) 240 4810.

The Romantic Novelists' Association. Offers probationary membership to unpublished romantic novelists, conditional on being prepared to submit a full length ms to be considered for the Netta Muskett Award for New Writers. For full details of membership, contact Hon Secretary Joyce Bell, Cobble Cottage, 129 New

Street, Baddesley Ensor, Nr Atherston, Warwickshire CV9 2DL. Tel: (01827) 714776.

The Scottish Association of Writers. Groups, clubs and workshops for writers throughout Scotland. Organises conferences, competitions and weekend schools for members. Membership open to any group of writers (no minimum number) forming a club/circle/workshop. Individual postal membership can be arranged. Details of membership and subscription rates from the President, Sheila Livingstone, 36 Cloan Crescent, Bishopbriggs, Glasgow G64 2HL. Tel: (0141) 772 5604.

The Theatre Writers' Union has been incorporated into the Writers' Guild of Great Britain. At the time of writing, it had not yet been decided whether or not the TWU's policy of offering membership to unpublished playwrights would continue. You can contact the Theatre Writers' Union at the Writers' Guild's address.

Services

CRITICISM AND MANUSCRIPT ASSESSMENT

Façade (the Façade Partnership of Richard Andrews and Mary Stewart-David) was founded in 1988 to create, promote and produce new works in musical theatre. Façade offers services ranging from an information base through casting to budgeting and general management. Façade also runs an introductory course called 'Making a Musical', on which Richard Andrews' book *Writing a Musical* is based. Other activities to help and encourage new writers and composers include Readers' Reports, workshops and showcases. For more details, contact Richard Andrews, Façade, 43A Garthorne Road, London SE23 1EP. Tel: (0181) 699 8655.

Flair for Words. An organisation run specifically to help new and semi-professional writers, but numbers many professionals among its membership. The proprietors, Cass and Janie Jackson, are dedicated to helping writers realise their ambitions, and offer a number of ways of doing so. Their services include a bi-monthly publication, *Flair Newsletter*, which gives inspiration, encouragement, guidance and market information, 'Flair Comments', a critique service, handbooks covering specific topics, and information audio cassettes. For full details of services and annual subscription, contact Cass and Janie Jackson, 5 Delavall Walk, Eastbourne BN23 6ER.

The London School of Journalism. Undertakes criticism and editing of full-length novels, memoirs, biographies and other literary works. Three forms of criticism are offered:
1. A general report and opinion.
2. A more detailed and constructive criticism with suggested revision.
3. Complete editing of a manuscript.
   The fees will depend on which service you choose. Details from The Secretary, The London School of Journalism, 22 Upbrook

Mews, Bayswater, London W2 3HG. Tel: (0171) 706 3536.

National Poetry Foundation will give appraisals of your poems as part of the benefits öf membership, which costs £20 per annum. Contact the founder, Johnathon Clifford, National Poetry Foundation, 27 Mill Road, Fareham, Hampshire PO16 0TH. Tel: (01329) 822218.

Oriel Critical Service for Writers (for writers living in Wales only). This service is supported by the Welsh Arts Council. It offers constructive advice based on a close reading of submitted work, and gives rigorous and detailed criticism. For full details of the service and current fees, contact Oriel Critical Service, Oriel Bookshop, The Friary, Cardiff CF1 4AA.

The Penman Criticism Service. Membership of the Penman Club entitles you to criticism of mss at no further charge. See page 162.

The Poetry Society Critical Service. Founded by Norman Hidden. Professional experts provide detailed reports on poetry. For full details, contact the Administrator, Poetry Society Critical Service, 22 Betterton Street, London WC2H 9BU. Tel: (0171) 240 4810. Fax: (0171) 240 4818.

Radio and Television Script Criticism Service. Rosemary Horstmann offers expert criticism and tuition, either to individuals or to groups, by arrangement. See Chapter 12. Contact Rosemary Horstmann, 122 Mayfield Court, West Savile Terrace, Edinburgh EH9. Tel: (0131) 667 1377.

The Writers Advice Centre offers critiques, workshops, talks, courses, writers' holidays. Run by Nancy Smith, Jane Baker and Louise Jordan. For details, send an SAE to Jasmine Cottage, Church Road, Brean, Burnham-on-Sea, Somerset TA8 2SF. Tel: (01278) 751316.

PUBLISHING

Author-Publisher Network (A-PN). A self-help and support association for self-publishers, offering shared marketing and joint distribution arrangements, seminars, workshops, bookfairs and promotional events. For details, contact the Press Officer, John Beasley, South Riding, 6 Everthorpe Road, London SE15 4DA.

Book-in-Hand Ltd. A print production service for self-publishers. The service includes design and editing advice, to give self-publishers a better chance of selling their work to the public. Run by Ann Kritzinger, a widely experienced and award-winning champion of self-publishing. Book-in-Hand Ltd, 20 Shepherds

Hill, London N6 5AH. Tel/Fax: (0181) 341 7650.

INFORMATION SERVICES AND SOURCES

Book Trust. A marvellous source of information on all things literary: prizes, publications, exhibitions, readings, books in print and so on. For details of all Book Trust services, send an SAE (6.5 x 9 inches) to The Publicity Officer, Book Trust, Book House, 45 East Hill, London SW18 2QZ. Tel: (0181) 870 9055.

British Library Newspaper Library, Colindale Avenue, London NW9 5HE. Tel: (0171) 412 7353. Fax: (0171) 412 7379.

French's Theatre Bookshop (Samuel French Ltd) is an excellent source of books and cassettes on all the media and performing arts, including writing. They'll send you lists on request (it helps if you can specify your area/s of interest). French's operate a comprehensive mail order service. Details from French's Theatre Bookshop, 52 Fitzroy Street, London W1P 6JR. Tel: (0171) 387 9373.

Greeting Card and Calendar Association is a professional association of greeting card companies. Where possible, they'll try to help with individual enquiries about their members' requirements. Contact The Information Officer, Greeting Card and Calendar Association, 6 Wimpole Street, London W1M 8AS. Tel: (0171) 637 7692. The Association's monthly magazine *Greetings* is available on subscription. Contact Lema Publishing Co, Unit No. 1, Queen Mary's Avenue, Watford, Hertfordshire WD1 7JR. Tel: (01923) 250909.

Literary research service. All subjects, but specialising in biography, and police and criminal history (including associated political and social effects). Other literary services, including 'ghosting', are available. Contact Rod Richards, 'Tracking Line', 23 Spearhill, Lichfield, Staffordshire WS14 9UD. Tel: (01543) 254748.

Network Scotland Ltd. An information broker delivering high quality information on a broad range of subjects. A leaflet detailing services can be obtained on request. For general information and information about education and training services, contact Network Scotland Ltd, 57 Ruthven Lane, The Mews, Glasgow G12 9JQ. Tel: (0141) 357 1774.

NIACE (The National Institute of Adult Continuing Education, England and Wales). Publishes (twice a year) the booklet *Residential Short Courses*, £4.95 post paid. Contact NIACE, 21 De Montford Street, Leicester LE1 7GE. Tel: (0116) 255 1451.

Oriel, The Welsh Arts Council's Bookshop. Offers a variety of services to writers and small and new publishers; as well as the Writers' Critical Service for writers living in Wales, there's a regular programme of literary events, an ad hoc advice service to small and new publishers looking for ways to market their publications, a regularly updated address list of small presses and little magazines, and a mail order service selling books about books and writing. Details of all Oriel's services and their book lists from Peter Finch, Oriel Bookshop, The Friary, Cardiff CF1 4AA.

Photographic agency: Popperfoto, Paul Popper Limited, The Old Mill, Overstone Farm, Northampton NN6 0AB. Tel: (01604) 670670. Fax: (01604) 670635.

The Poetry Library. For information on anything concerning poetry: publications, competitions, events. Royal Festival Hall, Level 5, London SE1 8XX. Tel: (0171) 921 0943/0664/0940. Fax: (0171) 921 0939.

LITERARY AGENTS

Dorian Literary Agency (Dorothy Lumley), Upper Thornehill, 27 Church Road, St Marychurch, Torquay, Devon TQ1 4QY. Tel: (01803) 312095.

Midland Exposure (Lesley Gleeson and Cari Crook), 4 Victoria Court, Oadby, Leicester LE2 4AF. (Short fiction for women's magazines.)

CORRESPONDENCE COURSES

The Academy of Children's Writers Ltd, PO Box 95, Huntingdon, Cambridgeshire PE17 5RL.

The College of Technical Authorship (Principal, John Crossley), PO Box 7, Cheadle, Cheshire SK8 3BY. Tel/Fax: (0161) 437 4235. E-mail: crossley@coltecha.u-net.com

London School of Journalism, 22 Upbrook Mews, Bayswater, London W2 3HG. Tel: (0171) 706 3536.

POSTAL WORKSHOPS

The Cottage Guide to Postal Workshops lists writing workshops countrywide conducted by post. Contact Mrs Catherine M Gill, Drakemyre Croft, Cairnorrie, Methlick, Ellon, Aberdeenshire AB41 0JN (£2 post paid).

SEMINARS AND RESIDENTIAL COURSES

The Arvon Foundation runs residential courses at three centres, two in England and one in Scotland: Lumb Bank, Heptonstall, Hebden Bridge, West Yorkshire HX7 6DF. Tel: (0170 681) 6582, Totleigh Barton, Sheepwash, Devon EX21 5NS, and Moniack Mhor, Inverness-shire IV4 7HT.

Swanwick Writers' Summer School. An annual six-day event, usually held in August. Top writers (many with very famous names) run courses and give lectures. Early booking is advisable. Contact the Secretary, Mrs Brenda Courtie, The New Vicarage, Parsons Street, Woodford Halse, Daventry, Northamptonshire NN11 3RE. Tel: (01327) 61477.

Writers' Holiday in Wales. A week-long holiday/conference held annually in the last week of July, usually at Caerleon College in South Wales. A packed programme of courses, lectures, seminars, workshops and so on, with many of our top writers and tutors participating. Full details and booking form from D L Anne Hobbs, 30 Pant Road, Newport, Gwent NP9 5PR. Tel/Fax: (01633) 854 976.

See also **NIACE** directory of residential courses (page 166).

More Useful Addresses

PROFESSIONAL ASSOCIATIONS

The Arts Council of Great Britain, 14 Great Peter Street, London SW1P 3NQ. Tel: (0171) 333 0100.

British Broadcasting Corporation (BBC), Broadcasting House, Portland Place, London W1A 1AA. Tel: (0171) 580 4468.

National Council for the Training of Journalists (NCTJ), Latton Bush Centre, Southern Way, Harlow, Essex CM18 7BL. Tel: (01279) 430009. Fax: (01279) 438008.

National Union of Journalists (NUJ), Acorn House, 314 Gray's Inn Road, London WC1X 8DP. Tel: (0171) 278 7916. Fax: (0171) 837 8143.

The Newspaper Society, Bloomsbury House, 74-77 Great Russell Street, London WC1B 3DA. Tel: (0171) 636 7014. Fax: (0171) 631 5119.

The Society of Authors, 84 Drayton Gardens, London SW10 9SB. Tel: (0171) 373 6642. Fax: (0171) 373 5768.

Workers' Educational Association (WEA), National Office, Temple House, 17 Victoria Park Square, London E2 9PB. Tel: (0181) 983 1515. Fax: (0181) 983 4840.

The Writers' Guild of Great Britain, 430 Edgware Road, London W2 1EH. Tel: (0171) 723 8074. Fax: (0171) 706 2413.

PUBLISHERS MENTIONED IN THE TEXT

Allison & Busby, 114 New Cavendish Street, London W1M 7FD. Tel: (0171) 0636 2530.

Andersen Press Ltd, 20 Vauxhall Bridge Road, London SW1V 2SA. Tel: (0171) 973 9720. Fax: (0171) 233 6263.

Aurum Press Ltd, 25 Bedford Avenue, London WC1B 3AT. Tel: (0171) 637 3225. Fax: (0171) 580 2469.

Bantam Press – an imprint of Transworld Publishers Ltd.

B T Batsford Ltd, 483 Fulham Road, London SW6 5AU. Tel: (0171)

471 1100.

BBC Books, 80 Wood Lane, London W12 0TT. Tel: (0181) 576 2000. Fax: (0181) 749 8766.

A & C Black (Publishers) Ltd, 35 Bedford Row, London WC1R 4JH. Tel: (0171) 242 0946. Fax: (0171) 831 8478.

Bloomsbury Publishing Plc, 2 Soho Square, London W1V 6HB. Tel: (0171) 494 2111. Fax: (0171) 434 0151.

Brimax Books Ltd, 4-5 Studlands Park Industrial Estate, Exning Road, Newmarket, Suffolk CB8 7AU. Tel: (01638) 664611. Fax: (01638) 665220.

Jonathan Cape Ltd, Random House, 20 Vauxhall Bridge Road, London SW1V 2SA. Tel: (0171) 973 9730. Fax: (0171) 233 6117.

Cambridge University Press, The Edinburgh Building, Shaftesbury Road, Cambridge CB2 2RU. Tel: (01223) 312393. Fax: (01223) 315052.

Cassell, Wellington House, 125 Strand, London WC1R 0BB. Tel: (0171) 420 5555. Fax: (0171) 240 7261.

Kyle Cathie Ltd, 20 Vauxhall Bridge Road, London SW1V 2SA. Tel: (0171) 973 9710. Fax: (0171) 821 9258.

Child's Play International, Ashworth Road, Bridgemead, Swindon, Wiltshire SN5 7YD. Tel: (01793) 616286. Fax: (01793) 512795.

Christian Focus Publications, Geanies House, Fearn, Tain, Rossshire, Scotland IV20 1TW. Tel: (01862) 87541. Fax: (01862) 87699.

T & T Clark, 59 George Street, Edinburgh EH2 2LQ. Tel: (0131) 225 4703. Fax: (0131) 220 4260.

Constable & Co Ltd, 3 The Lanchesters, 162 Fulham Palace Road, London W6 9ER. Tel: (0181) 741 3663. Fax: (0181) 748 7562.

The Crowood Press Ltd, The Stable Block, Crowood Lane, Ramsbury, Marlborough, Wiltshire SN8 2HR.

Darton, Longman & Todd Ltd, 1 Spencer Court, 140-142 Wandsworth High Street, London SW18 4JJ. Tel: (0181) 875 0155. Fax: (0181) 875 0133.

Dorling Kindersley Ltd, 9 Henrietta Street, London WC2E 8PS. Tel: (0171) 836 5411. Fax: (0171) 836 7570.

Elliott Right Way Books, Kingswood Buildings, Lower Kingswood, Tadworth, Surrey KT20 6TD. Tel: (01737) 832202. Fax: (01737) 830311.

Epworth Press, c/o Methodist Publishing House, 20 Ivatt Way, Peterborough, Cambridgeshire PE3 7PG. Tel: (01733) 332202. Fax: (01733) 331201.

Faber & Faber Ltd, 3 Queen Square, London WC1N 3AU. Tel: (0171) 465 0045. Fax: (0171) 465 0034.

W Foulsham & Co, The Publishing House, Bennetts Close, Cippenham, Berkshire SL1 5AP. Tel: (01753) 526769. Fax: (01753) 535003.

Samuel French Ltd, 52 Fitzroy Street, London W1P 6JR. Tel: (0171) 387 9373. Fax: (0171) 387 2161.

Victor Gollancz, Wellington House, 125 Strand, London WC2R 0BB. Tel: (0171) 420 5555. Fax: (0171) 240 7261.

Robert Hale Ltd, Clerkenwell House, 45-47 Clerkenwell Green, London EC1R 0HT. Tel: (0171) 251 2661. Fax: (0171) 490 4958.

Hamlyn, Michelin House, 81 Fulham Road, London SW3 6RB. Tel: (0171) 581 9393. Fax: (0171) 225 9528.

HarperCollins Publishers Ltd, 77–85 Fulham Palace Road, London W6 8JB. Tel: (0181) 741 3200. Fax: (0181) 306 3119.

Headline, 338 Euston Road, London NW1 3BH. Tel: (0171) 873 6000. Fax: (0171) 873 6024.

Heinemann, Michelin House, 81 Fulham Road, London SW3 6RB. Tel: (0171) 581 9393. Fax: (0171) 225 9095.

Hodder & Stoughton, 338 Euston Road, London NW1 3BH. Tel: (0171) 873 6000. Fax: (0171) 873 6024.

How To Books Ltd, 3 Newtec Place, Magdalen Road, Oxford OX4 1RE. Tel: (01865) 793806. Fax: (01865) 248780.

Kogan Page Ltd, 120 Pentonville Road, London N1 9JN. Tel: (0171) 278 0433. Fax: (0171) 837 3768/6348.

Legend, Random House, 20 Vauxhall Bridge Road, London SW1V 2SA. Tel: (0171) 973 9700. Fax: (0171) 233 6127.

Lion Publishing, Peter's Way, Sandy Lane West, Oxford OX4 5HG. Tel: (01865) 747550. Fax: (01865) 747568.

Little, Brown & Co (UK), Brettenham House, Lancaster Place, London WC2E 7EN. Tel: (0171) 911 8000. Fax: (0171) 911 8100.

Macmillan Publishers Ltd, 25 Eccleston Place, London SW1W 9NF. Tel: (0171) 881 8000. Fax: (0171) 881 8001.

Methuen, Michelin House, 81 Fulham Road, London SW3 6RB. Tel: (0171) 581 9393. Fax: (0171) 589 9095.

Mills & Boon (Harlequin Mills & Boon Ltd), Eton House, 18–24 Paradise Road, Richmond, Surrey TW9 1SR. Tel: (0181) 948 0444. Fax: (0181) 288 2899.

Mulholland-Wirral, The Croft, School Avenue, Little Neston, South Wirral L64 4BS. (Telephone unlisted.)

New English Library, 338 Euston Road, London NW1 3BH. Tel: (0171) 873 6000. Fax: (0171) 873 6024.

Oxford University Press, Walton Street, Oxford OX2 6DP. Tel: (01865) 56767. Fax: (01865) 56646.

Penguin Books Ltd, 27 Wrights Lane, London W8 5TZ. Tel: (0171) 416 3000. Fax: (0171) 416 3099.

Piatkus Books, 5 Windmill Street, London W1P 1HF. Tel: (0171) 631 0710. Fax: (0171) 436 7137.

Random House Ltd, Random House, 20 Vauxhall Bridge Road, London SW1V 2SA. Tel: (0171) 973 9000. Fax: (0171) 233 6058.

Robinson Publishing, 7 Kensington Church Court, London W8 4SP. Tel: (0171) 938 3830. Fax: (0171) 938 4214.

Scholastic Ltd, Villiers House, Clarendon Avenue, Leamington Spa, Warwickshire CV32 5PR. Tel: (01926) 887799. Fax: (01926) 883331.

Serpent's Tail, 4 Blackstock Mews, London N4 2BT. Tel: (0171) 354 1949. Fax: (0171) 704 6467.

Swan Hill Press, Airlife Publishing Ltd, 101 Longden Road, Shrewsbury, Shropshire SY3 9EB. Tel: (01743) 235651. Fax: (01743) 232944.

Thames & Hudson Ltd, 30-34 Bloomsbury Street, London WC1B 3QP. Tel: (0171) 636 5488. Fax: (0171) 636 4799.

D C Thomson & Co Ltd, Albert Square, Dundee DD1 9QJ. Tel: (01382) 23131. Fax: (01382) 22214.

Thorsons, 77-85 Fulham Palace Road, London W6 8JB. Tel: (0181) 741 7070. Fax: (0181) 307 4440.

Transworld Publishers Ltd, 61-63 Uxbridge Road, London W5 5SA. Tel: (0181) 579 2652. Fax: (0181) 579 5479.

Viking, 27 Wrights Lane, London W8 5TZ. Tel: (0171) 416 3000. Fax: (0171) 416 3099.

Vintage, Random House, 20 Vauxhall Bridge Road, London SW1V 2SA. Tel: (0171) 973 9700. Fax: (0171) 233 6127.

Virgin Publishing, 332 Ladbroke Grove, London W10 5AH. Tel: (0181) 968 7554. Fax: (0181) 968 0929.

Walker Books Ltd, 87 Vauxhall Walk, London SE11 5HJ. Tel: (0171) 793 0909. Fax: (0171) 587 1123.

J Whitaker & Sons Ltd, 12 Dyott Street, London WC1A 1DF. Tel: (0171) 836 8911. Fax: (0171) 836 2909.

The Women's Press, 34 Great Sutton Street, London EC1V 0DX. Tel: (0171) 251 3007. Fax: (0171) 608 1938.

Writer's Digest Books, 1507 Dana Avenue, Cincinnati, Ohio 45207, USA.

THEATRE COMPANIES

Liverpool Playhouse, Williamson Square, Liverpool L1 1EL. Tel:

(0151) 709 8478. Fax: (0151) 709 7113.
Paines Plough, 4th Floor, 43 Aldwych, London WC2B 4DA. Tel:
(0171) 240 4533. Fax: (0171) 240 4534.
Traverse Theatre, Cambridge Street, Edinburgh EH1 2ED. Tel:
(0131) 228 3223. Fax: (0131) 229 8443.

GREETING CARD COMPANIES

Graphic Humour, 4 Britannia Centre, Point Pleasant, Wall End,
Tyne & Wear NE28 6HQ.
Hanson-White-Accord, 9th Floor, Wettern House, 56 Dingwall
Road, Croydon, Surrey CR0 0XH. Tel: (0181) 680 1885. Fax:
(0181) 760 0093.
Paperlink Ltd, 59-61 Palfrey Place, London SW8 1AR. Tel: (0171)
582 8244.
Paper House Group, Shepherd Road, Gloucester, Gloucestershire
GL2 6EL. Tel: (01452) 423451. Fax: (01452) 410312.
United Greeting Card Co (UK) Ltd, River Park, Billet Lane,
Berkhamsted, Hertfordshire HP4 1EL. Tel: (01442) 871381.

OTHER RELEVANT ORGANISATIONS

Arts Council of Northern Ireland, 185 Stranmills Road, Belfast BT9
5DU. Tel: (01232) 381591. Fax: (01232) 661715.
Arts Council of Wales, Museum Place, Cardiff CF1 3NX. Tel:
(01222) 394711. Fax: (01222) 221447.
Association of Authors' Agents, c/o Greene & Heaton Ltd, 37
Goldhawk Road, London W12 8QQ. Tel: (0181) 749 0315. Fax:
(0181) 749 0318.
British Copyright Council, Copyright House, 29-33 Berners Street,
London W1P 4AA. Contact the Secretary.
Children's Book Circle, c/o Orchard Books, 96 Leonard Street,
London EC2A 4RH. Tel: (0171) 739 2929. Fax: (0171) 739 2318.
Crime Writers Association, PO Box 10772, London N6 4RY.
Membership restricted to professional crime writers (fiction or
non-fiction) but associate membership available to publishers,
literary agents and booksellers who specialise in crime.
Guild of Erotic Writers, PO Box 381, Selsdon Way, London E14
9GL. Tel: (0171) 987 5090. Fax: (0171) 538 3690. A network for all
authors of erotic fiction, both published and unpublished.
Legal Deposit Office, The British Library, Boston Spa, West
Yorkshire LS23 7BY. Tel: (01937) 546267. Fax: (01937) 546586.

Public Lending Right Office, Bayheath House, Prince Regent Street, Stockton-on-Tees, Cleveland TS18 1DF Tel: (01642) 604699.

Scottish Arts Council, 12 Manor Place, Edinburgh EH3 7DD. Tel: (0131) 226 6051.

Society of Civil Service Authors, 4 Top Street, Wing, Nr Oakham, Rutland LE15 8SE. Membership Secretary Mrs Joan Hykin.

Society of Freelance Editors and Proofreaders (SFEP), c/o SFEP Office, 38 Rochester Road, London NW1 9JJ. Tel: (0171) 813 3113.

Society of Indexers, 38 Rochester Road, London NW1 9JJ. Tel: (0171) 916 7809. Secretary Claire Troughton.

Society of Women Writers and Journalists, Hon Secretary Jean Hawkes, 110 Whitehall Road, Chingford, London E4 6DW.

Women Writers Network, 23 Prospect Road, London NW2 2JU. Tel: (0171) 794 5861.

Further Reading

BOOKS FOR WRITERS

Art of Romance Writing, The, Valerie Parv (Allen & Unwin, 1993) pb £7.99.

Author's Guide to Publishing, An, Michael Legat (Hale, 1991) £6.95.

Bestseller, Celia Brayfield (Fourth Estate, 1996) £7.99.

Bloody Murder, Julian Symons (Penguin, revised edn 1985) pb £3.95.

Book Book, The, Anthony Blond (Cape, 1985) hb £9.95.

Book Writer's Handbook, The, Gordon Wells (Allison & Busby, 3rd edn 1996/97) pb £7.99.

Bring It To Book, Ann Kritzinger (Scriptmate, 1997) pb £8.99.

Complete Book of Feature Writing, The, Ed. Leonard Witt (Writer's Digest Books, 1991) hb $18.95*.

Complete Guide to Writing Fiction, The, Ed. Barnaby Conrad (Writer's Digest Books, 1990) hb $18.95*.

Copy-editing, Judith Butcher (Cambridge University Press, 3rd edn 1992) hb £19.95.

Copyright & Law for Writers, Helen Shay (How To Books, 1996) pb £8.99.

Craft of Copywriting, The, Alastair Crompton (Century Hutchinson 1987) pb £6.95.

Craft of Lyric Writing, The, Sheila Davis (Writer's Digest Books, 1986) hb $18.95*.

Craft of Writing Articles, The, Gordon Wells (Allison & Busby, 1983) pb £8.99.

Craft of Writing Poetry, The, Alison Chisholm (Allison & Busby, 1992) pb £8.99.

Craft of Writing Romance, The, Jean Saunders (Allison & Busby, 1988) pb £8.99.

Craft of Writing Science Fiction That Sells, The, Ben Bova (Writer's Digest Books, 1996) hb $16.99*.

Creating a Twist in the Tale, Adele Ramet (How To Books, 1996) pb £8.99.

Do Your Own Advertising, Alastair Crompton (Century Hutchinson, 1987) pb £6.95.

Doing Business on the Internet, Graham Jones (How To Books, 1997) pb £12.99.

Editing for Print, Geoffrey Rogers (Macdonald, 1986) hb £9.95.

Freelance Writing for Newspapers, Jill Dick (A & C Black, 1991) pb £9.99.

Freelancing for Magazines, John Morrison (Bureau of Freelance Photographers, 1991) hb £12.95.

Getting into Print, Jenny Vaughan (Bedford Square Press, 1988) pb £4.95.

Guide to Fiction Writing, Phyllis Whitney (Poplar Press, 1984) pb £4.95.

Guide to Self-Publishing – The A-Z of Getting Yourself into Print, Harry Mullholland (Mullholland-Wirral, 1984) pb £6.95 + £1 p&p direct from the publisher – see page 68.

How Poetry Works, Philip Davies Roberts (Pelican, 1986) pb £3.95.

How to Compile and Sell Crosswords and Other Puzzles, Graham R Stevenson (Allison & Busby, 1997) pb £8.99.

How to Create Fictional Characters, Jean Saunders (Allison & Busby, 1996) pb £6.99.

How to Draw and Sell Comic Strips, Alan McKenzie (Macdonald Orbis, 1988) hb £12.95.

How to Publish a Book, Robert Spicer (How To Books, 2nd edn 1996) pb £9.99.

How to Publish Your Poetry, Peter Finch (Allison & Busby, new edn July 1998) pb £8.99.

How to Publish Yourself, Peter Finch (Allison & Busby, new edn Dec 1997) pb £8.99.

How to Research Your Novel, Jean Saunders (Allison & Busby, 1993) pb £6.99.

How to Sell Every Magazine Article You Write, Lisa Collier Cool (Writer's Digest Books, 1986) hb $14.95*.

How to Use the Internet, Graham Jones (How To Books, 1996) pb £9.99

How to Write a Miffion, Ansen Dibell, Orson Scott Card and Lewis Turco (Robinson, 1996) pb £9.99.

How to Write a Play for the Amateur Stage, Dilys Gater (Allison & Busby, 1991) pb £4.99.

How to Write & Illustrate Children's Books, Bicknell & Trotman (Writer's Digest Books, 1988) hb $23.99*.

How to Write & Sell Greeting Cards, Bumper Stickers, T-Shirts and

Other Fun Stuff, Molly Wigand (Writer's Digest Books, 1992) pb $15.95*.

How to Write and Sell Your First Novel, Oscar Collier with Frances Spatz Leighton (Writer's Digest Books, 1986) pb $12.95*.

How to Write Five-Minute Features, Alison Chisholm (Allison & Busby, 1996) pb £8.99.

How to Write for Children, Tessa Krailing (Allison & Busby, 1988) pb £8.99.

How to Write for Religious Markets, Brenda Courtie (Allison & Busby, 1996) pb £8.99.

How to Write for Television, William Smethurst (How To Books, 1992) pb £8.99.

How to Write Non-Fiction Books, Gordon Wells (Allison & Busby, 1996) pb £8.99.

How to Write Realistic Dialogue, Jean Saunders (Allison & Busby, 1995) pb £6.99.

How to Write Short-Short Stories, Stella Whitelaw (Allison & Busby, 1996) pb £8.99.

Inside Book Publishing, Giles N Clark (Blueprint, 1988) hb £12.95.

Insider's Guide to Writing for Screen and Television, Ronald Tobias (Writer's Digest Books) pb $17.99*.

Internet for Dummies, The, Levine, Baroudi & Young (IDG Books, 1995) £16.99.

Journalism for Beginners, Joan Clayton (Piatkus, 1992) pb £7.99.

Magazine Journalism Today, Anthony Davis (Heinemann, 1988) pb £12.95.

Magazine Writer's Handbook, The, Gordon Wells (Allison & Busby, 1997) pb £8.99.

Metric Feet & Other Gang Members, Johnathon Clifford, 1994 (£6 from The National Poetry Foundation, cheques payable to 'Johnathon Clifford').

Photography for Article Writers, Gordon Wells (Allison & Busby, 1991) pb £4.99.

Plotting & Writing Suspense Fiction, Patricia Highsmith (Poplar Press, 1983) pb £4.95.

Practical Picture Research, Hilary Evans. (New edition £39 + £3 p&p from Mary Evans Picture Library, 1 Tranquil Vale, Blackheath, London SE3 0BU. Tel: (0181) 318 0034.)

Practical Poetry Course, A, Alison Chisholm (Allison & Busby, 1996) pb £8.99.

Professional Etiquette for Writers, William Brohaugh (Writer's Digest Books, 1986) hb $9.95*.

Rough Guide to the Internet & World Wide Web, The, Angus J Kennedy (Rough Guides Ltd, 1996) pb £5.

Songwriters' Market, Ed. Cindy Laufenbery (Writer's Digest Books, annual pubn.) hb $22.99*.

Songwriting, Stephen Citron (Hodder & Stoughton, 1987) hb £14.95.

Starting to Write, Marina and Deborah Oliver (How To Books, 1996) pb £8.99.

Successful Author's Handbook, The, Gordon Wells (Papermac) pb £7.99.

Teach Yourself Copywriting, J Jonathan Gabay (Hodder & Stoughton Teach Yourself Books, 1996) pb £7.99.

30-Minute Writer, The, Connie Emerson (Writer's Digest Books, 1993) pb $14.99*.

To Writers With Love, Mary Wibberley (Buchan & Enright, 1987) pb £4.95.

Travel Writing: A Guide to Research, Writing & Selling, L Peat O'Neil (Writer's Digest Books) hb $19.99*.

Way to Write for Children, The, Joan Aiken (Elm Tree, 1982) pb £6.95.

Writer's Companion, The, Barry Turner (Macmillan, 1996) pb £12.99.

Writers' Questions Answered, Gordon Wells (Allison & Busby) pb £6.99.

Writer's Rights, The, Michael Legat (A & C Black) pb £9.99.

Writing a Musical, Richard Andrews (Hale, 1997) pb £9.99.

Writing a Nonfiction Book, Norman Toulson (How To Books, 1997) pb £9.99.

Writing a Novel, John Braine (Methuen, 1974) pb £6.99.

Writing a Play, Steve Gooch (A & C Black) pb £9.99.

Writing a Textbook, Penny Grubb and Danuta Reah (How To Books, 1997) pb £12.99.

Writing About Travel, Morag Campbell (A & C Black, 1989) pb £8.99.

Writing & Selling a Novel, Marina Oliver (How To Books, 1996) pb £8.99.

Writing Below the Belt, Michael Rowe (Masquerade Books, USA, 1995) hb £17.99.

Writing Business, The, Liz Taylor (Severn House, 1985 – out of print, but worth searching for) pb £3.95.

Writing Crime Fiction, H R F Keating (A & C Black, 1986) pb £8.99.

Writing Erotic Fiction, Derek Parker (A & C Black, 1995) pb £8.99.

Writing Feature Articles, Brendan Hennessy (Heinemann, 1989) pb £12.95.

Writing for Children, Margaret Clark (A & C Black, 1993) pb £7.99.

Writing for Magazines, Jill Dick (A & C Black, 1994) pb £9.99.

Writing for Pleasure and Profit, Michael Legat (Hale, 1986) pb £4.99.

Writing for Radio, Rosemary Horstmann (A & C Black, 1991) pb £9.99.

Writing for the Teenage Market, Ann de Gale (A & C Black) pb £8.99.

Writing for Young Children, Claudia Lewis (Poplar Press, 1984) pb £4.95.

Writing Reviews, Carol Baldock (How To Books, 1996) pb £9.99.

Writing Romantic Fiction, Marina Oliver (How To Books, 1997) pb £9.99.

Writing Science Fiction, Fantasy & Horror, Christopher Kenworthy (How To Books, 1997) pb £9.99.

Writing Step By Step, Jean Saunders (Allison & Busby, 1986) pb £5.99.

Writing the Novel From Plot to Print, Lawrence Block (Writer's Digest Books, 1979) pb $9.95*.

Writing to Inspire, William Gentz and Lee Roddy (Writer's Digest Books, 1986) pb $14.95*.

*The prices of the American Writer's Digest Books listed are given in US dollars, to give you an idea of their cost. Many of these books are now available through larger UK bookshops. You can buy them direct from Writer's Digest Books, 1507 Dana Avenue, Cincinnati, Ohio 45207, USA. Write for prices and information on ordering from outside the USA.

MAGAZINES AND NEWSPAPERS MENTIONED IN THE TEXT

The Beano, The Dandy, My Weekly, Mandy & Judy, People's Friend and *Twinkle* are all published by D C Thomson & Co Ltd, Albert Square, Dundee DD1 9QJ. Tel: (01382) 23131. Fax: (01382) 22214.

Bella, Shirley House, 25-27 Camden Road, London NW1 9LL. Tel: (0171) 284 0909. Fax: (0171) 485 3774.

Best, 197 Marsh Wall, London E14 9SG. Tel: (0171) 519 5500. Fax: (0171) 519 5516.

Catholic Herald, Lamb's Passage, Bunhill Row, London EC1Y 8TQ. Tel: (0171) 588 3101. Fax: (0171) 256 9728.

Church Times, 33 Upper Street, London N1 0PN. Tel: (0171) 359 4570. Fax: (0171) 226 3073.

Hello!, Wellington House, 69-71 Upper Ground, London SE1 9PQ. Tel: (0171) 334 7404. Fax: (0171) 334 7412.

Jewish Chronicle, 25 Furnival Street, London EC4A 1JT. Tel: (0171) 405 9252. Fax: (0171) 405 9040.

New Christian Herald, Herald House, 96 Dominion Road, Worthing, West Sussex BN14 8JP. Tel: (01903) 821082. Fax: (01903) 821081.

Practical Photography, Apex House, Oundle Road, Peterborough, Cambridgeshire PE2 9NP. Tel: (01733) 898100. Fax: (01733) 894472.

Private Eye, 6 Carlisle Street, London W1V 5RG. Tel: (0171) 437 4017. Fax: (0171) 437 0705.

Stage and Television Today, The, 47 Bermondsey Street, London SE1 3XT. Tel: (0171) 403 1818. Fax: (0171) 403 1418.

The Tablet, 1 King Street Cloisters, Clifton Walk, London W6 0QZ. Tel: (0181) 748 8484. Fax: (0181) 748 1550.

Take a Break, Shirley House, 25-27 Camden Road, London NW1 9LL. Tel: (0171) 284 0909. Fax: (0171) 284 3778.

Woman's Weekly, King's Reach Tower, Stamford Street, London SE1 9LS. Tel: (0171) 261 5000. Fax: (0171) 261 6322.

PUBLICATIONS OF PARTICULAR INTEREST TO NEW WRITERS

Acumen, editor Patricia Oxley, 6 The Mount, Higher Furzeham, Brixham, Devon TQ5 8QY. Current subscription rates on request (please enclose an SAE).

American Markets Newsletter, monthly, editor Sheila O'Connor. Newsletter giving a wide range of American markets not covered in the conventional reference books. For subscription details, send an SAE to Sheila O'Connor, 175 Westland Drive, Glasgow G14 9JQ.

The Author, editor Derek Parker. The official magazine of The Society of Authors. Available to non-members on subscription. Current rates from the Publications Department, The Society of Authors, 84 Drayton Gardens, London SW10 9SB. Tel: (0171) 373 6642.

Book and Magazine Collector, editor Crispin Jackson. Monthly from newsagents or by subscription. Current rates on request from Book and Magazine Collector, 43-45 St Mary's Road, Ealing, London W5 5RQ. Tel: (0181) 579 1082.

The Bookseller, 'the organ of the book trade', editor Louis Baum. Weekly, to order through newsagents or by subscription. Current rates from The Bookseller, J Whitaker & Sons, 12 Dyott Street, London WC1A 1DF. Tel: (0171) 420 6000.

The Deansgate Portfolio (Alien Landings) is a showcase magazine for new short stories in the science fiction, fantasy and horror genres. For details and writers' guidelines, send an SAE to the Science Fiction Desk, Waterstone's Booksellers, 91 Deansgate, Manchester M3 2BW. Tel: (0161) 832 1992. Fax: (0161) 835 1534.

Envoi (poetry only), editor Roger Elkin. Three issues per year. Subscription rates on application (please enclose an SAE) from Envoi, 44 Rudyard Road, Biddulph Moor, Stoke-on-Trent, Staffordshire ST8 7JN. Tel: (01782) 517892.

First Time (poetry only), editor Josephine Austin. Two issues a year. For current subscription rates, please send an SAE to Josephine Austin, Burdett Cottage, George Street, Old Town, Hastings, East Sussex TN23 3ED.

Flair Newsletter, editors Cass and Janie Jackson. The newsletter from Flair for Words, a support system for writers. For details of the newsletter and other services, send an SAE to Flair for Words, 5 Delavall Walk, Eastbourne, East Sussex BN23 6ER.

Greetings is the magazine of the Greeting Card and Calendar Association. Monthly, subscription UK £30, Europe £40, elsewhere £50 per annum. From Lema Publishing Co, Unit No 1, Queen Mary's Avenue, Watford, Hertfordshire WD1 7JR. Tel: (01923) 250909. Fax: (01923) 250995.

Helicon, Peninsular, Reach and *Writers' Express* are magazines published by Cherrybite Publications. They cover articles, competitions, poetry and short stories. For details, send an SAE to editor/publisher Shelagh Nugent, Cherrybite Publications, Linden Cottage, 45 Burton Road, Little Neston, South Wirral, Merseyside L64 4AE.

Metropolitan, editors Elizabeth Baines and Ailsa Cox, is a stylish bi-annual magazine publishing quality literary short stories. Potential contributors are strongly advised to read at least one copy before submitting mss. *Metropolitan* is on sale in quality bookshops in cities and larger towns (£3.50 per copy) and is also available on subscription. For details, please send an SAE to Metropolitan Magazine, 19 Victoria Avenue, Manchester M20 2GY.

The New Writer, editor Suzanne Ruthven. SAE, please, for ordering details and contributors' guidelines, PO Box 60, Cranbrook, Kent TN17 2ZR.

Outposts Poetry Quarterly, editor Roland John. SAE for subscription rates to 22 Whitewell Road, Frome, Somerset BA11 4EL.

Publishing News, editor Fred Newman. Weekly newspaper of the book trade. For details, contact Publishing News, 43 Museum Street, London WC1A 1LY. Tel: (0171) 404 0304. Fax: (0171) 242 0762.

QWF (Quality Women's Fiction), editor Jo Good. Quarterly small press magazine for women's short-story writing. SAE for details to 80 Main Street, Swadlincote, Derbyshire DE12 6QA.

Stand Magazine, editors Jon Silkin and Lorna Tracy. Quarterly literary fiction and poetry magazine. SAE for details to 179 Wingrove Road, Newcastle upon Tyne, NE4 9DA. Tel: (0191) 273 3280.

Writers' Bulletin, editors Chriss McCallum and John Benton. Monthly (except August and January). Markets, resources, competitions, information and news, all verified at source. For details, send an SAE. For details and a sample back issue, send 4 second-class postage stamps to Chriss McCallum, Writers' Bulletin, PO Box 96, Altrincham, Cheshire WA14 2LN.

Writers' Forum, editor Morgan Kenney. Articles on writing and photo-journalism, competitions, seminars, workshops. For details and a sample copy send £1 in postage stamps to Writers' Forum, 21 Belle Vue Street, Filey, North Yorkshire YO14 9HU.

Writers' Guide, editor Geoff Carroll. Details from 11 Shirley Street, Hove, East Sussex BN3 3WJ.

Writers' News, editor Richard Bell. Monthly magazine for writers, with articles, competitions, market news. Subscribers also receive the bi-monthly news-stand magazine *Writing* at no extra charge. Details from PO Box 4, Nairn IV12 4HU, Scotland. Tel: (01667) 454441. Fax: (01667) 454401.

Writer's Own Magazine, editor Mrs Eileen M Pickering. Quarterly. SAE for details, please, to Mrs E M Pickering, 121 Highbury Grove, Clapham, Bedford MK41 6DU.

Cassette

'*And then he kissed her...*' £9.95 post paid from Mills & Boon Ltd, Reader Service, PO Box 236, Thornton Road, Croydon, Surrey CR9 3RU.

American magazines

The Writer, monthly. Introductory rates offered to new subscribers. For details of current subscription rates and offers, send an IRC to The Writer Inc, 120 Boylston Street, Boston, MA 02116 4615, USA.

Writer's Digest, monthly. Like *The Writer* (above) offers special rates to new subscribers. IRC for details to Writer's Digest, 1507 Dana Avenue, Cincinnati, Ohio 45207, USA.

RECOMMENDED REFERENCE BOOKS

Chambers Dictionary (1993 edition) £22.50.

Dictionary of Literary Terms, Martin Gray (Longman York Handbooks, 1984) pb £2.95.

Learn to Type in 30 Days, Brenda Beaver (B Beaver, Salisbury, Wilts) hb course £6.95.

The Oxford Dictionary for Writers and Editors (Clarendon/OUP) hb £9.99.

Pears Cyclopedia (Pelham Books) hb £12.95.

Penguin Dictionary of Historical Slang, editor Eric Partridge (Penguin, 1973) £7.95.

Research for Writers, Ann Hoffmann (A & C Black) pb £9.99.

Roget's Thesaurus, various editions available.

Spell Well, compiled by Kirkpatrick and Schwartz (Chambers, 1980) hb £2.95.

Whitaker's Almanack (J Whitaker, Annual). Complete edition £22.50, shorter edition £11.95.

Write Right!, Jan Venolia (David & Charles, 1986) hb £4.95.

Writers' & Artists' Yearbook (A & C Black, annual) pb £11.99.

The Writer's Handbook, editor Barry Turner (Macmillan/Pen, annual) pb £12.50.

Consult these in the library
British Books in Print (J Whitaker).
Cassell's Media Directory (Cassell).
Willing's Press Guide (Reed Information Services).

USEFUL BOOKLETS

Brief Guide to Self-Publishing, Ann Kritzinger. £2.50 post paid from Book-in-Hand, 20 Shepherds Hill, London N6 5AH.

Cottage Guide to Postal Workshops, £2 post paid from Mrs Catherine M Gill, Drakemyre Croft, Cairnorrie, Methlick, Ellon, Aberdeenshire AB41 0JN.

Directory of Writers' Circles, £5 post paid from Jill Dick, 'Oldacre', Horderns Park Road, Chapel-en-le-Frith, High Peak SK23 9SY. (Please make cheques *etc* payable to Laurence Pollinger Ltd.)

Writing Plays for Radio (BBC Radio Drama). Guidelines available from the Chief Producer (Plays) BBC Drama Department, 16 Langham Street, London W1A 1AA. (Enclose an A-4 size SAE.)

Light Entertainment Radio guidelines available from the Senior Producer, Scripts, (Light Entertainment Radio), BBC Broadcasting House, London W1A 1AA. (Enclose an A4-size SAE.)

The Society of Authors publishes a series of 'Quick Guides' (to Copyright, Literary Agents, Libel and so on). These are free to members, and available to non-members for a small charge. For current titles and prices, contact The Society of Authors, 84 Drayton Gardens, London SW10 9SB. Tel: (0171) 373 6642.

Theatre Writing Schemes (brochure) on request from the Drama Director, The Arts Council of Great Britain, 14 Great Peter Street, London SW1P 3NQ. Tel: (0171) 333 0100.

Index